HENNA NADEEM

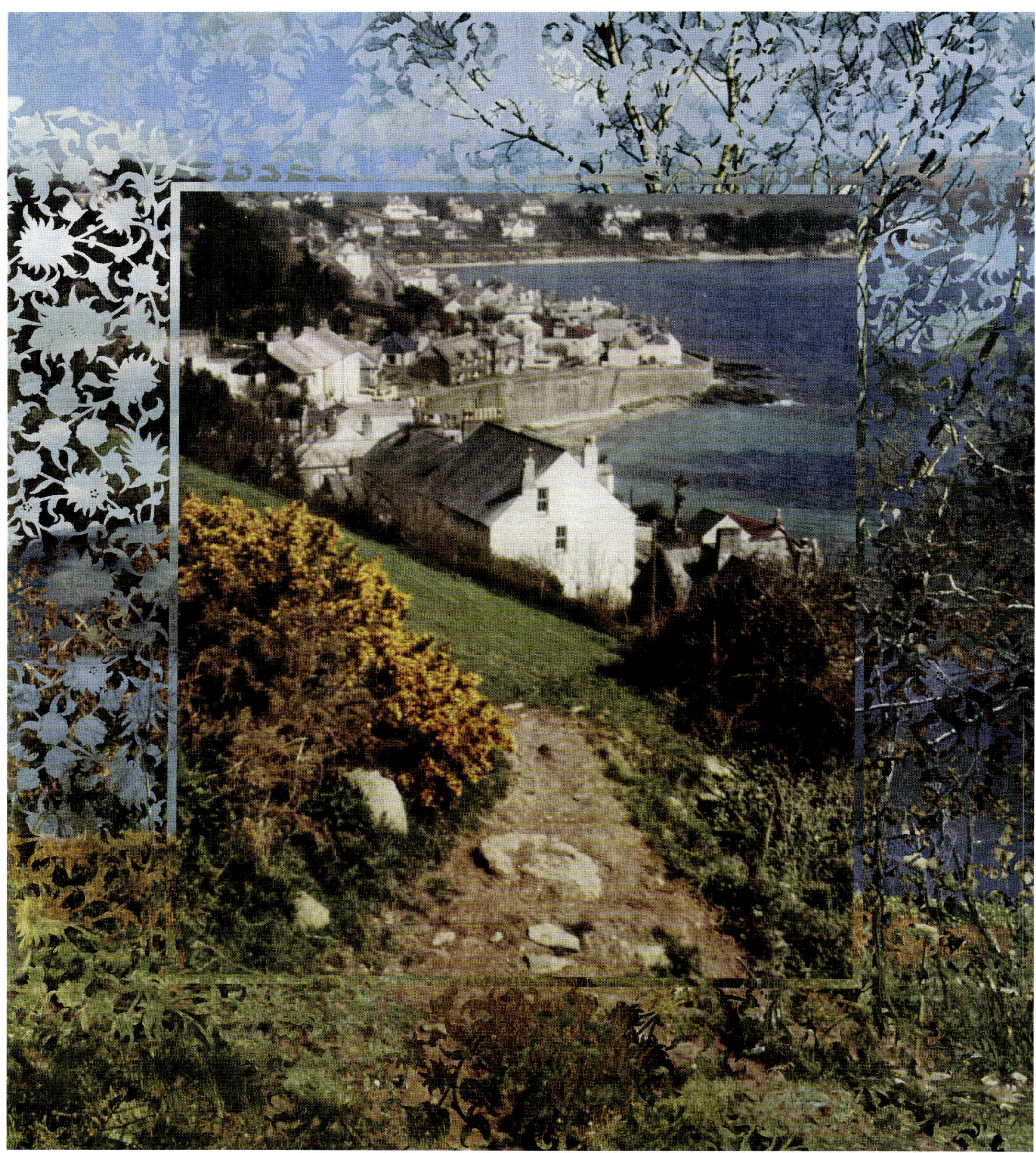

HENNA NADEEM

A PICTURE BOOK OF BRITAIN

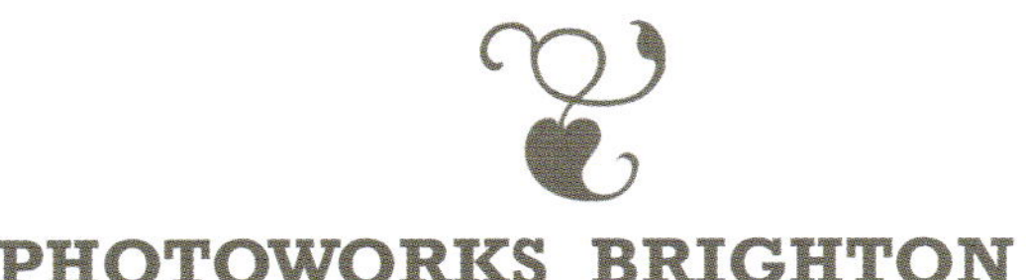
PHOTOWORKS BRIGHTON

'Viewed impressionistically from a distance the little town was still the jumble of small red-roofed houses and bungalows populated mostly by a comfortable retired middle class - but it was an impression that could not last more than a few minutes. Though the tiles still showed, the walls were barely visible. The tidy gardens had vanished under an unchecked growth of green, patched in colour here and there by the descendants of carefully-cultivated flowers. Even the roads looked like strips of green carpet from this distance. When we reached them we should find that the effect of soft verdure was illusory; they would be matted with course, tough weeds.'
John Wyndam, *The Day of the Triffids,* 1951

'England of the arterial by-pass, treeless and stinking of diesel oil, murderous with lorries; England of the bombing-range wherever there was once silence... England of high explosives falling upon the pre-historic monuments of Dartmoor. Barbaric England of the scientists, the military men and the politicians: let us turn away and contemplate the past before all is lost to the vandals.'
W.G.Hoskins, *The Making of the English Landscape,* 1955

'We are the Office Block Persecution Affinity / God save little shops, china cups and virginity / We are the skyscraper condemnation affiliate / God save tudor houses, antique tables and billiards / Preserving the old ways from being abused / Protecting the new ways for me and for you / What more can we do / God save the Village Green.'
The Kinks, *Village Green Preservation Society,* 1968

'We should not be deceived into thinking that this heritage is an acquisition, a possession that grows and solidifies; rather, it is an unstable assemblage of faults and fissures and heterogeneous layers that threaten the fragile inheritor from within or underneath... The search for descent is not the erecting of foundations: on the contrary, it disturbs what was previously considered immobile; it fragments what was thought unified; it shows the heterogeneity of what was imagined consistent with itself. What convictions and, far more decisively, what knowledge can resist it?'
Michel Foucault, *Nietzsche, Genealogy, History,* 1971

'The past lives on, in art and memory, but it is not static, it shifts and changes as the present throws its shadows backwards. The landscape also changes, but far more slowly; it is a living link between what we were and what we have become. This is one of the reasons we feel such profound and apparently disproportionate anguish when a loved landscape is altered out of recognition; we lose not only a place, but a part of ourselves, a continuity between the shifting phases of our life.'
Margaret Drabble, *A Writer's Britain: Landscape in Literature,* 1979

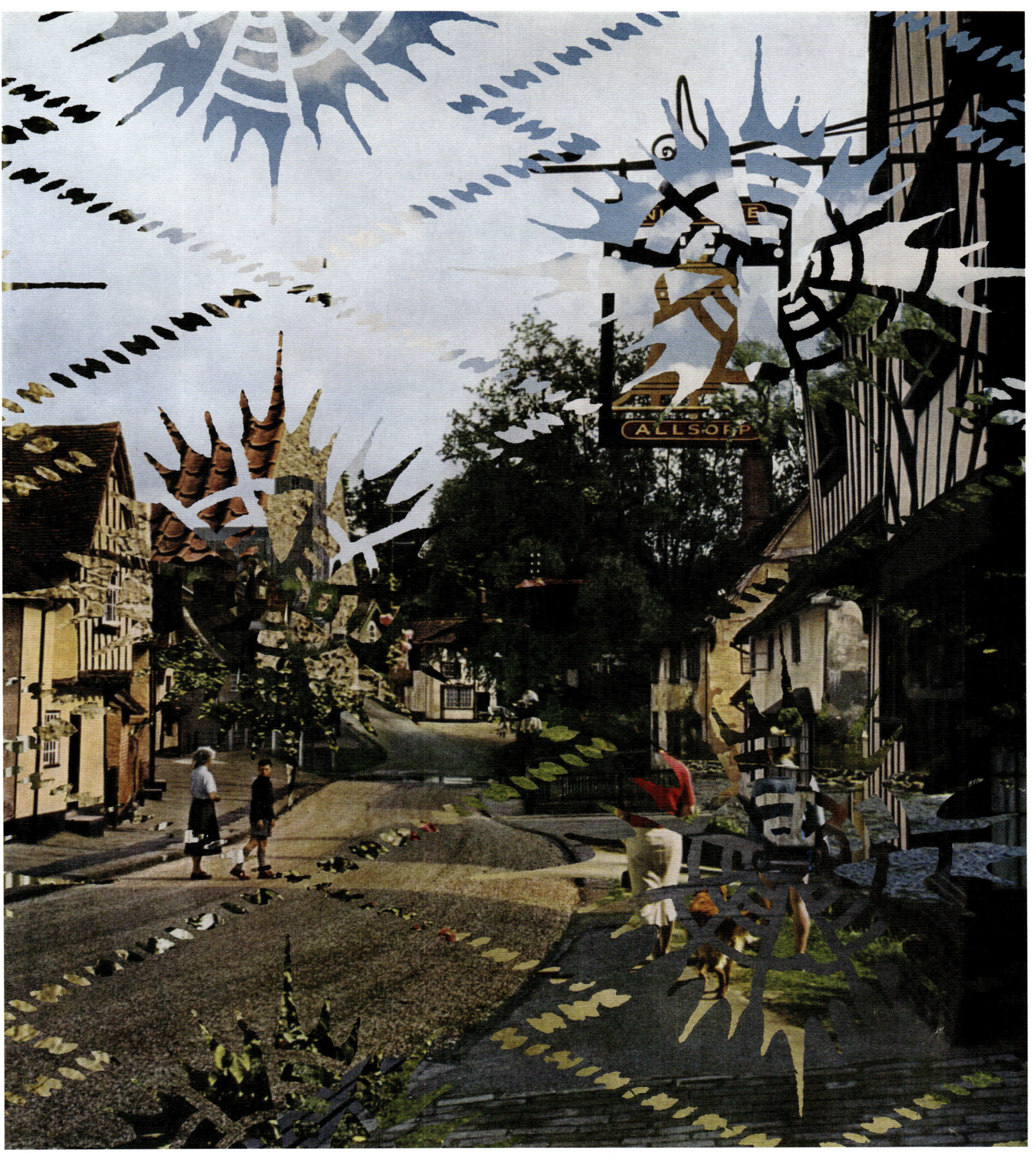
ALLSOPP

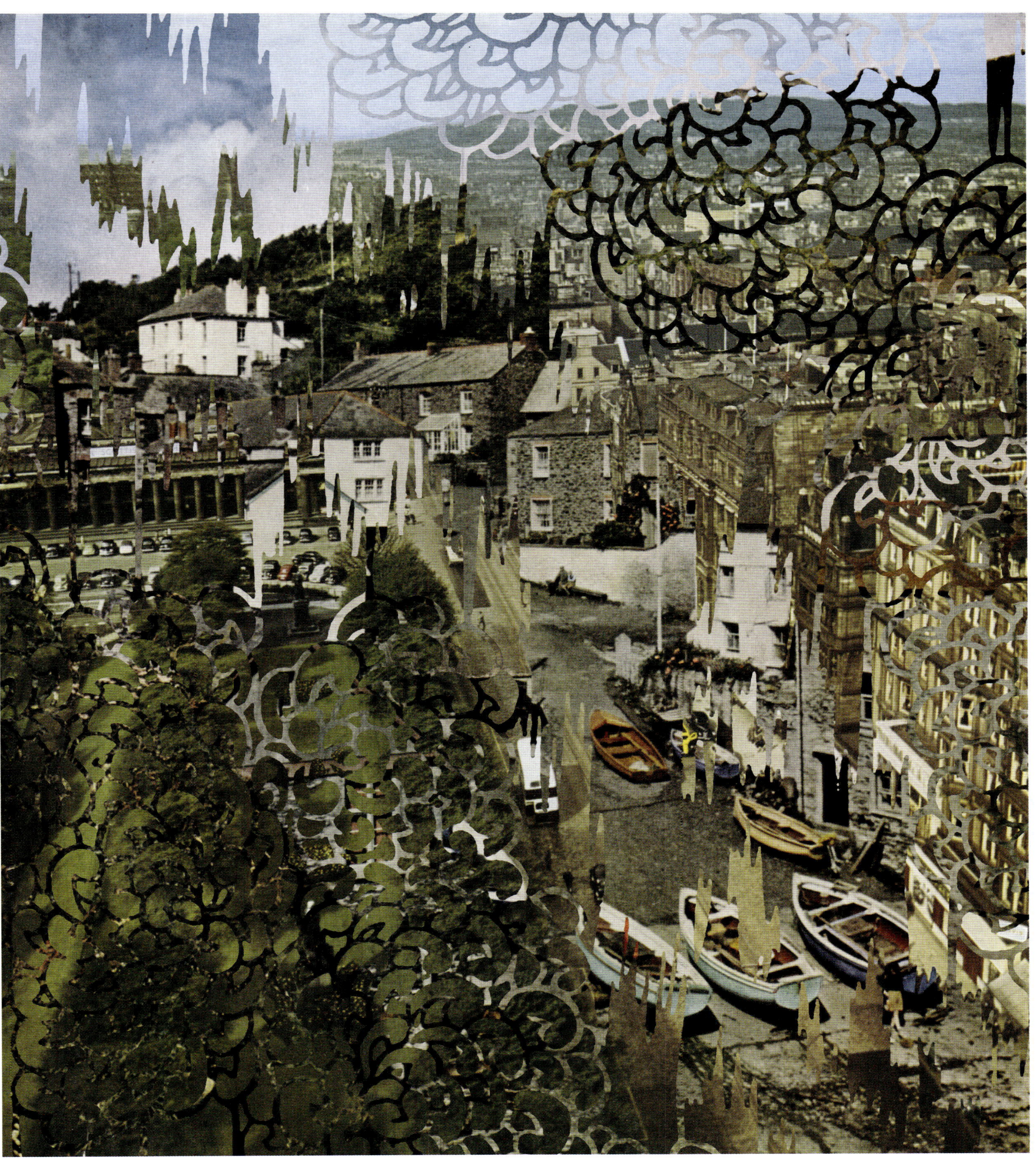

HENNA NADEEM
A PICTURE BOOK OF BRITAIN

David Chandler and Benedict Burbridge

This book is the product of a long and fruitful dialogue between Photoworks and the artist Henna Nadeem. It began, as many projects do, from a mixture of good intention and serendipity, which in this case involved an agreement with Henna to develop an artist's commission and the coincidental discovery of a book. The book in question was a 1966 edition of Country Life's *Picture Book of London*, bought by chance in a second hand bookshop for £2. In fact, discovery might be too strong a word – this book and others from what was a long-running series are not especially rare – but it was an exciting find for us, and a revelation, too, since the book contained exquisite and strange colour photographs of the city whose period reproduction lent them an even more surreal quality. With more research and more purchases a rough history of the books began to emerge.

First published in 1937, the *Picture Books of Britain* expanded through various series and later through various publishers, until the 1980s. They were in one sense travel companions, reflecting the growing popularity of tourism and tourist literature in the 1930s and the gradual 'opening-up' of the British countryside, something prompted in part by the expansion of the railways and the steady increase in car ownership. But the books were never practical guides, rather they were comprised of landscape 'views' that claimed to represent scenes typical of Britain's 'essential character' and as such were deemed 'pattern-books of Britain', templates for an ideal journey; as one book jacket put it: 'By turning the pages of this book the reader can indulge on an imaginary tour of the country'. Their wistful and nostalgic tone evidently struck a chord with the mood of the time because the books were very successful, often running to several editions and finding their place on respectable coffee tables and sideboards across the country where, although long replaced by other, glossier volumes, they live on in current memory.

Although in no sense groundbreaking as a publishing phenomenon or blessed with any distinctive artistic invention, the books and the photographs they contain are representative of a certain popular image of the British landscape that existed during this period. The books also reflect an important and enduring strand of the British imagination, one that sees our landscape, and particularly landscapes of this kind, as central to the idea of a national culture and identity. For many the books were not only a way of summarising Britain's 'essential character' but also a means of expressing solidarity with that character, of declaring membership to an essentially British club.

The Picture Books' deeply nostalgic vision gained additional currency as the prospect of war loomed – their romantic and unequivocal celebration of the land a stable and timeless image to set against what were for many the less palatable realities of a period of immense social change. After World War II the books were even more successful, chiming with a further retrenchment into Britain's past and traditions; the weary survival of bombed cities and continued rationing could be offset by the vision of a still untroubled rural Eden; as the book jacket to the reprinted Second Edition pronounced in 1947: 'Pictures such as these are part of our birthright... they will be welcomed more warmly than ever in a time of change, when more powerful means than the builder's pick and shovel have destroyed much that was dear.'

The Country Life books can be seen as part of a wider trend during the period centred on the preservation and packaging of a historic British past. This was embodied in

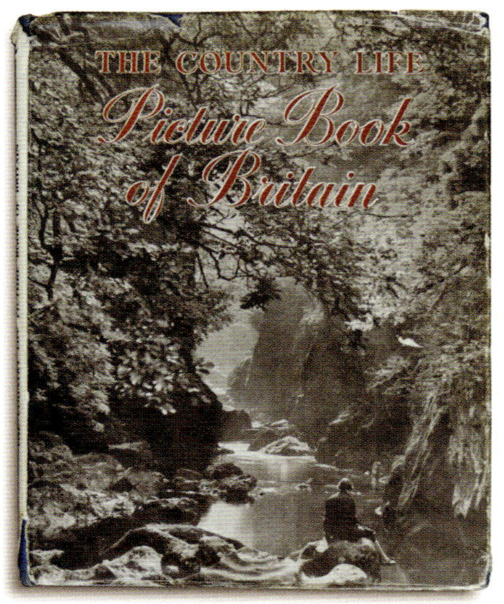

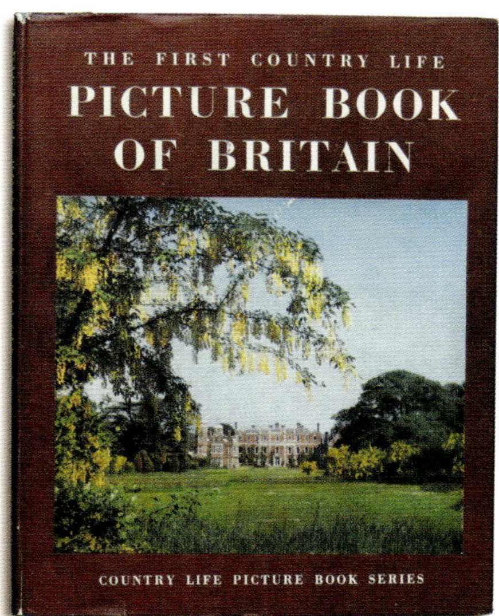

part by the growth of the 'heritage industries' and organizations such as the National Trust, whose role as chief protector of the nation's heritage was cemented in 1937 by the formation of the National Trust Act, and which by 1948, controlled 112,000 acres and nearly a hundred of Britain's historic buildings. Following the War, much of the country resigned itself to the necessity of extensive re-building, yet many feared that through this process of re-development something was also being irreparably destroyed. The growth of the conservation lobby and other bodies dedicated to the protection of the historic British landscape are obvious expressions of this concern and, in a modest way, the Country Life books also served as a vehicle for this anxiety. The photographs offered carefully selected portions of an archetypal Britain, shaping the country as a series of 'views' to be preserved against the 'encroachment' of modernisation and over-zealous town planners. The pictures envisage Britain as a series of 'places' that collectively make up a symbolic inventory of a landscape under threat, 'loved long since, and lost awhile.'

In many ways the photographers responsible for these pictures were following in the tradition of numerous artists before them, but they were now plying their romantic images with a moral currency derived from their particular historical circumstances. These were mostly 'scenic' photographers, either free-lance or agency-based people (and occasionally also seasoned explorers and writers) who travelled the country to capture its views, competing for subtlety, viewpoint and technical perfection in order to sell on their work to publishers such as Country Life for inclusion in their books and magazines. It is from this activity and a growing archive of photographs that the Picture Books' editors assembled their idealised vision of the British landscape, piecing together the cathedrals and mountainsides, villages and cliff tops, rolling hills and ancient forests, into a singular and lasting picture of the country's rural past.

Given this history, it soon became clear to us that the Picture Books were a potentially fertile source of imagery and ideas for Henna Nadeem, who since graduating from the Royal College of Art in 1993 has worked with found photographic images of the landscape. Henna often finds her material in books and magazines. She favours images that evoke strong Western pictorial traditions, traditions that have over centuries suggested the world's coherence, emphasising nature's benign power as something of an ideal space beyond the events of human history and civilisation. Then, in a process that begins to undermine the solidity of these images and ideas, she uses pattern templates derived from Islamic, Moorish and other non-Western sources as a basis for grafting images together into delicately interwoven collages. The mesmerising results of this process present a perceptual challenge to the viewer as two visual traditions collide and vie for prominence. There are obvious social and political implications in this, but Henna's work is not overtly polemical. Instead the act of subverting one dominant tradition with another is taken on with a certain grace and even playfulness as she relishes the new aesthetic possibilities of her collage technique, freely experimenting with a new hybrid language.

Photoworks commissions are usually conducted in relation to particular sites and contexts, the artist responding to conditions specific to that context. So in this case the Picture Books themselves would function as a site, giving a new focus to Henna's work and ideas, and, importantly, giving her the opportunity to extend her practice: firstly by working with an entire body of images and a specific conceptual framework; secondly by exploring the book form for the first time; and thirdly by allowing her the freedom to experiment with new skills and techniques. The idea for the commission that emerged from our discussions was that Henna should focus her attention on the colour editions of the Picture Books from the mid-sixties, where the images and the impressions of Britain they convey resonate strongly with her own personal history. Born in 1966, she grew up in what she calls 'semi-rural' Yorkshire, her parents having moved to Britain from Lahore in Pakistan along with many other south Asian families in the early sixties. They were the first non-white family in their village, an experience that has deeply affected Henna's sense of the landscape and its relationship to an enduring idea of Britishness. For Henna, the landscape remained somehow remote from her own existence, a framed spectacle viewed through her living room window along with the bewildering troops of hikers that made their way across the hillside on Sunday expeditions.

Drawing on these personal associations and aware of the books' broader cultural concerns, Henna has used the *Picture Books of Britain* as both practical and conceptual source material for her own pictures. Transforming their photographic reproductions into collages she has, for the first time, supplemented her hand cutting and pasting procedures with digital techniques that have substantially extended the range and possibilities of the work. The resulting images, collected in this book for the first time, respect the nostalgic quality of the original pictures and the strangely surreal impressions of the British countryside created by the colour separation process used in their printing. The work is both a homage and an intervention, reflecting the sense that our landscape and our past, as Margaret Drabble has suggested, 'are not static' but shift and change 'as the present throws its shadow backwards.'

Just as the Picture Books seemed to consciously offer the consolations of a heavenly place, increasingly unhinged from the particularities of actual locations or events, so Henna has pushed her work to new extremes and to powerful hallucinatory effect. In these collages 1960s Britain seems in the grip of parallel realities, not just an unstable, evolving place but one going through a gradual and at times nightmarish metamorphosis. As well as fitting evocations of the period, of cultural clashes and ever-diverging experiences existing side by side – and with a glance towards some of the most memorable graphic art of that time with its own non-Western affiliations – Henna's extraordinary works claim a space for an unheard generation, for children growing up and finding their voice. It is this blend of child-like innocence and knowing subversion that gives the artist's work its critical tension and the series in this book its particular poignancy.

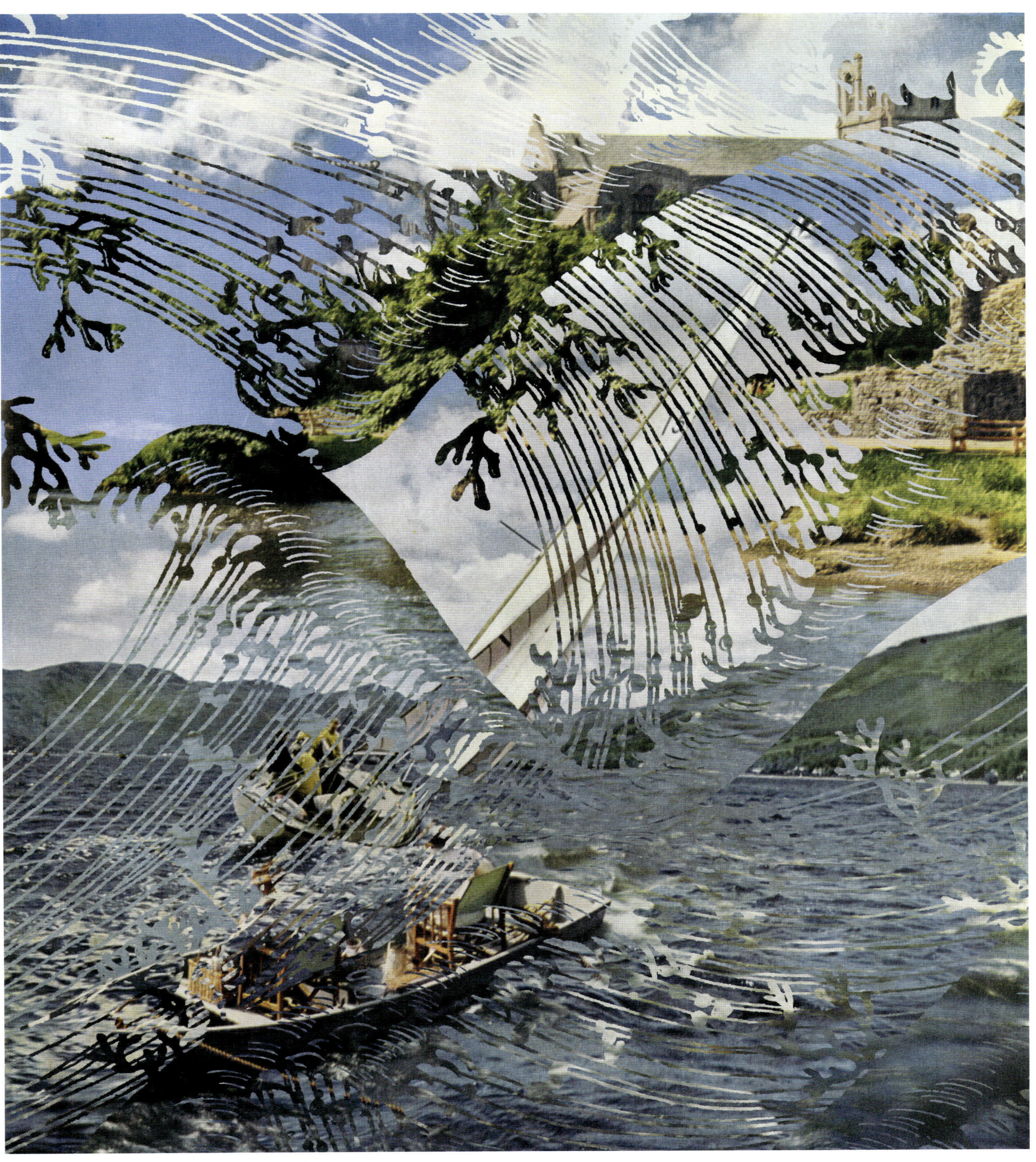

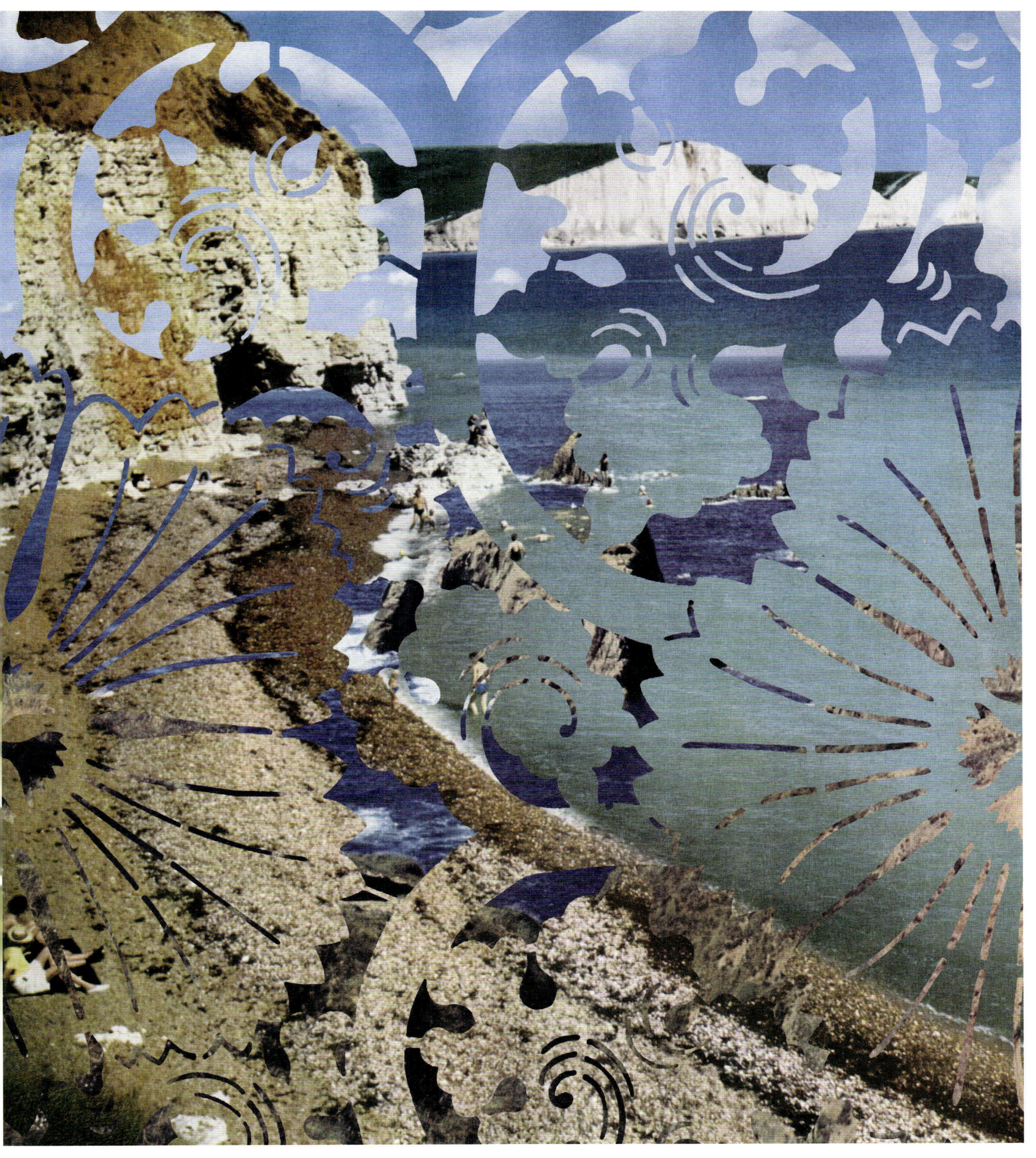

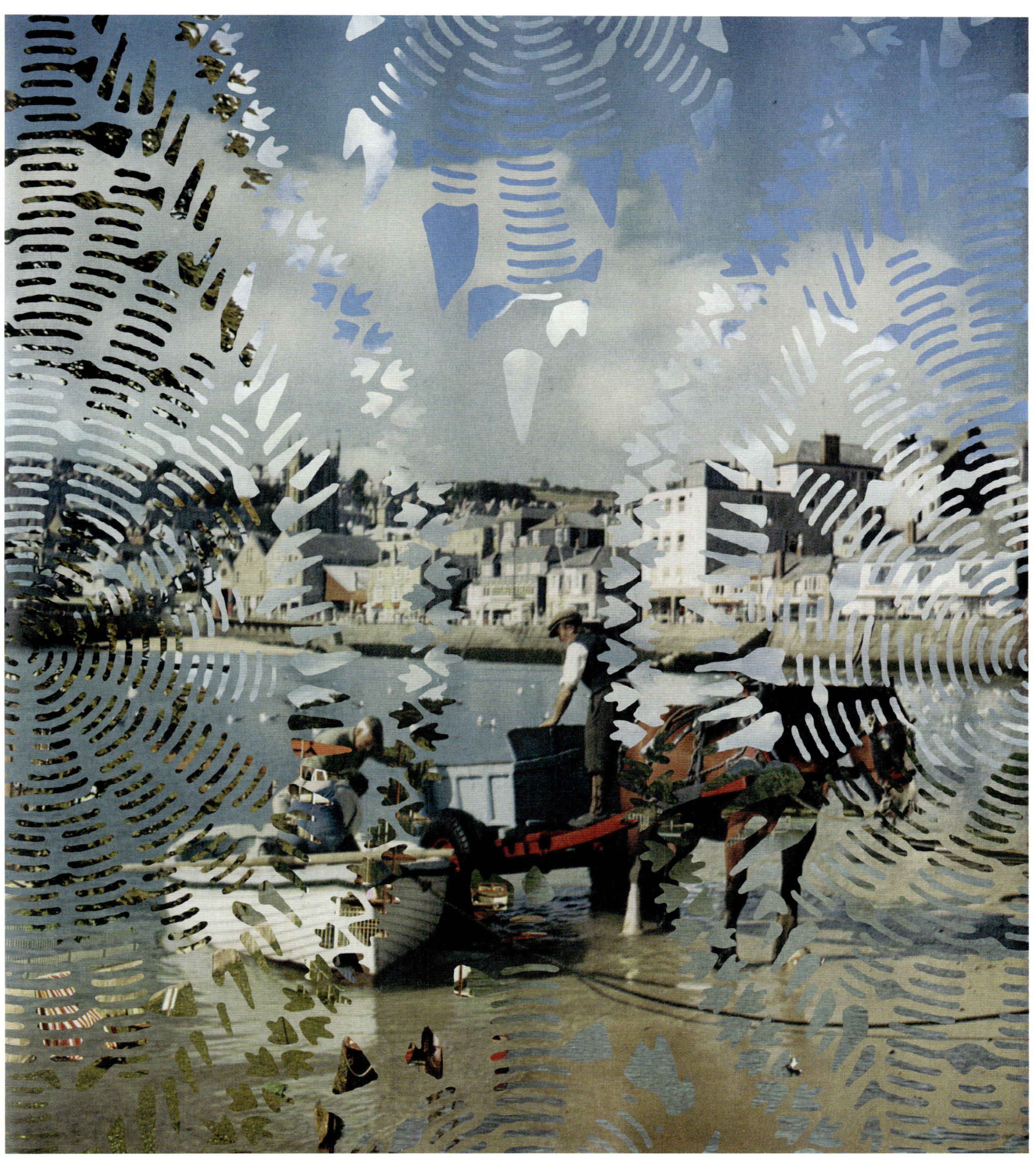

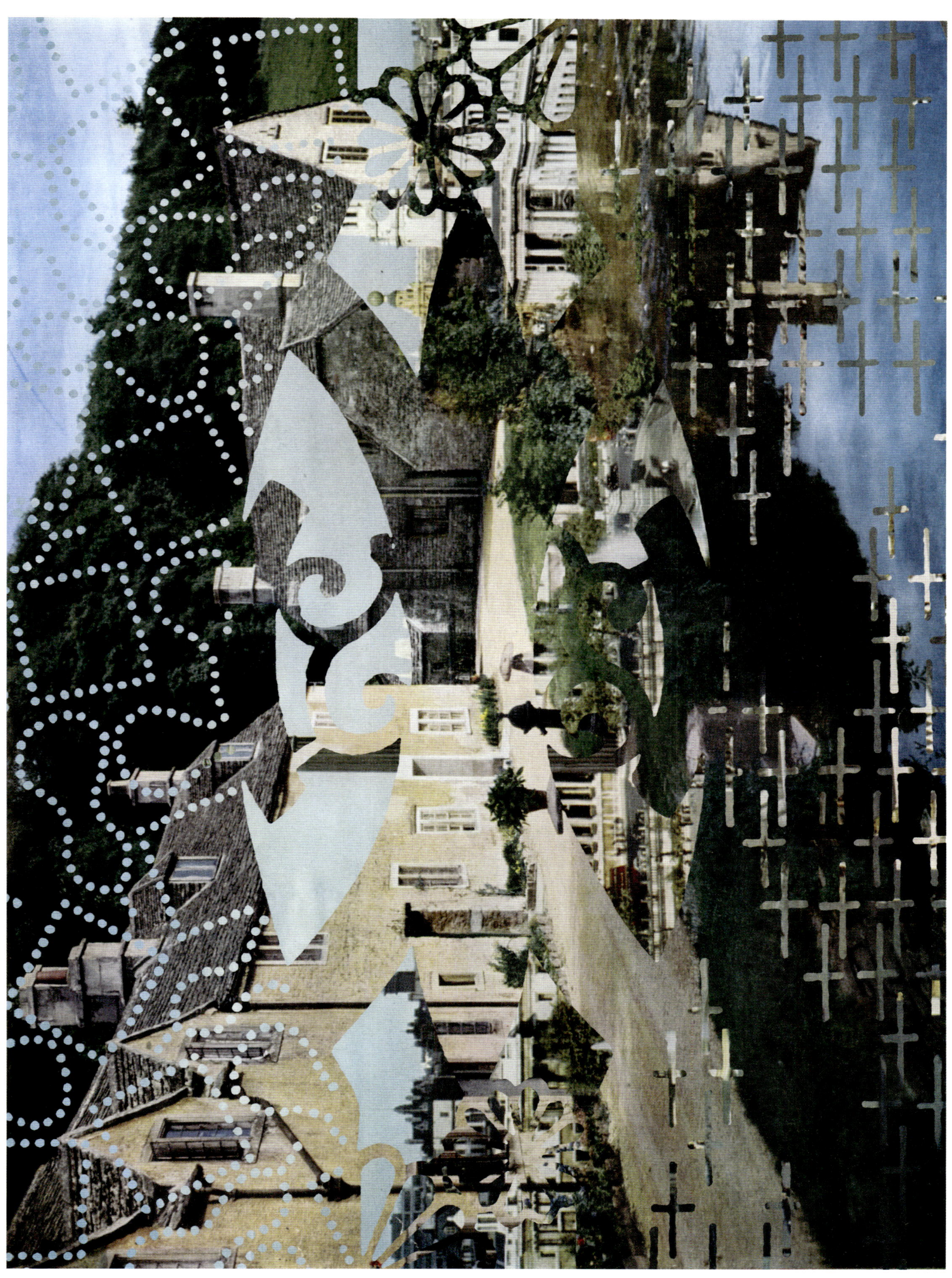

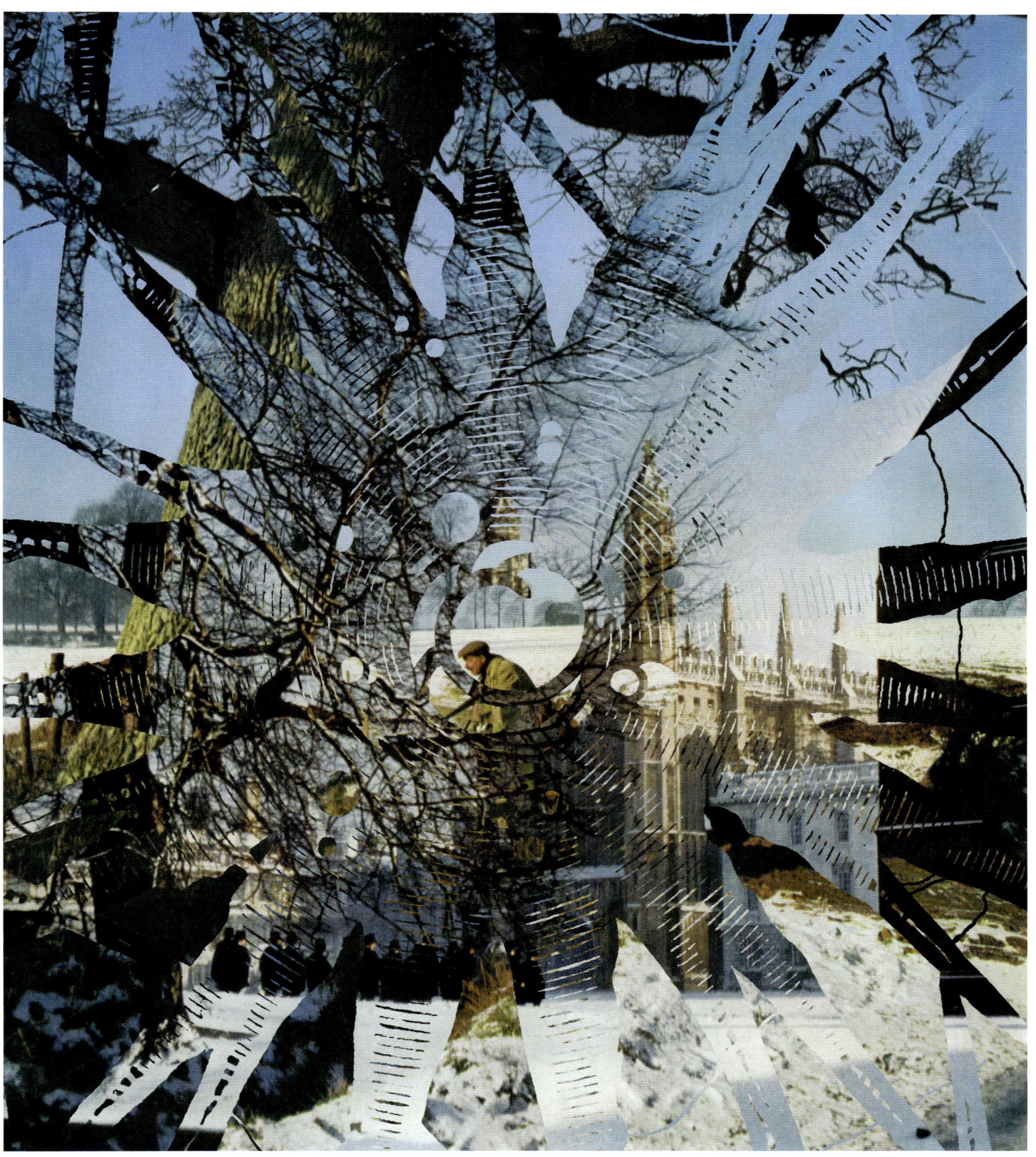

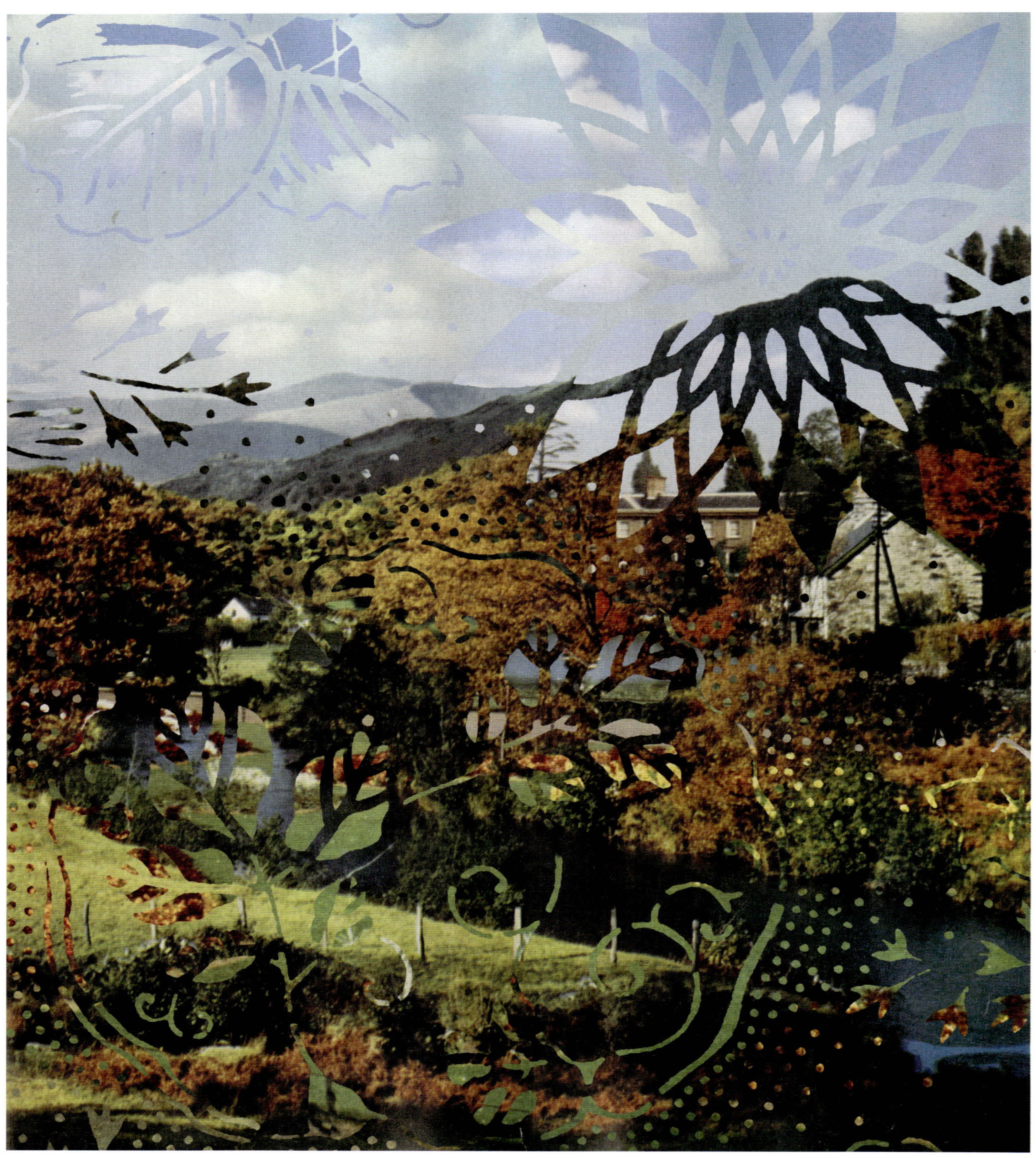

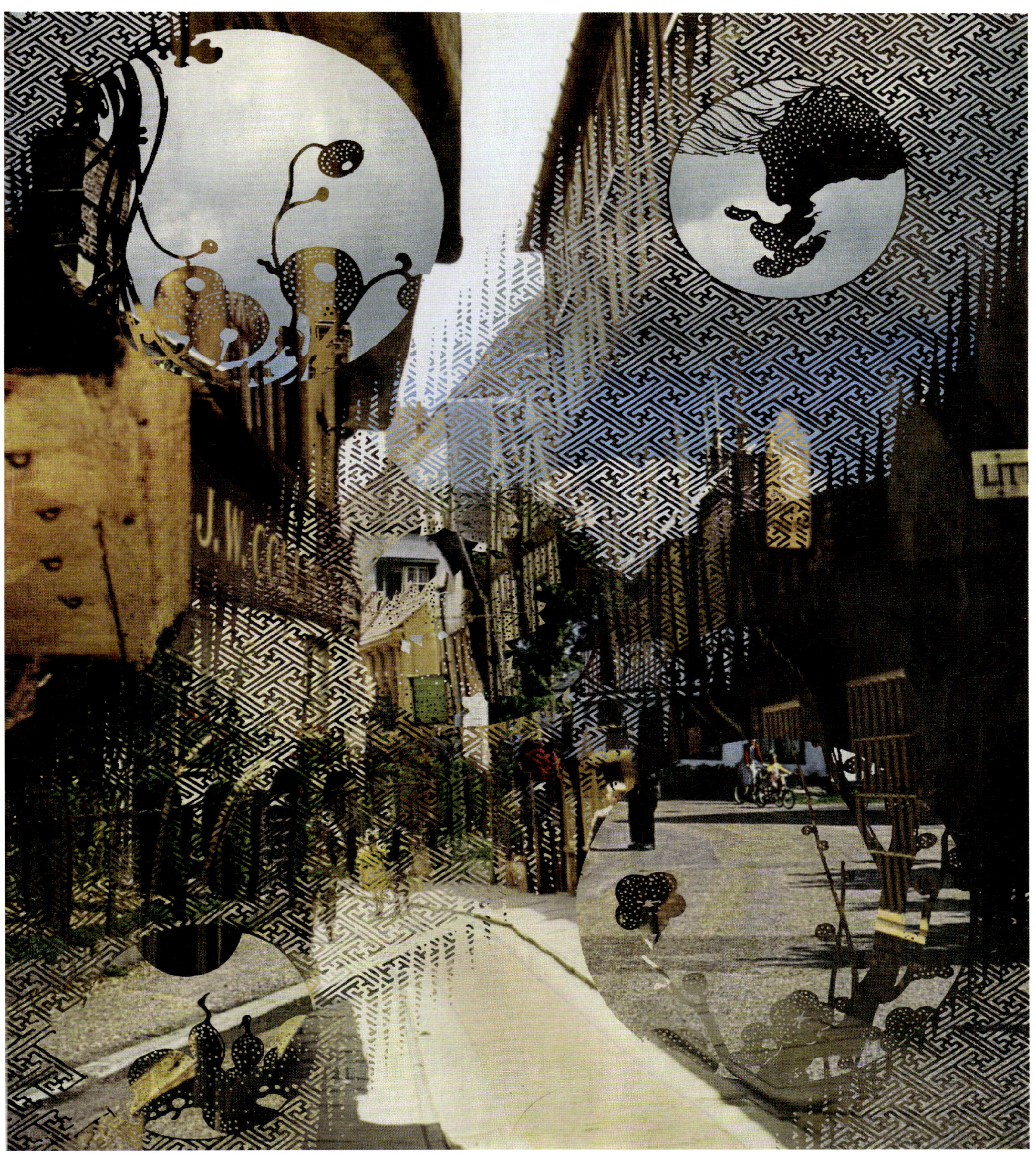

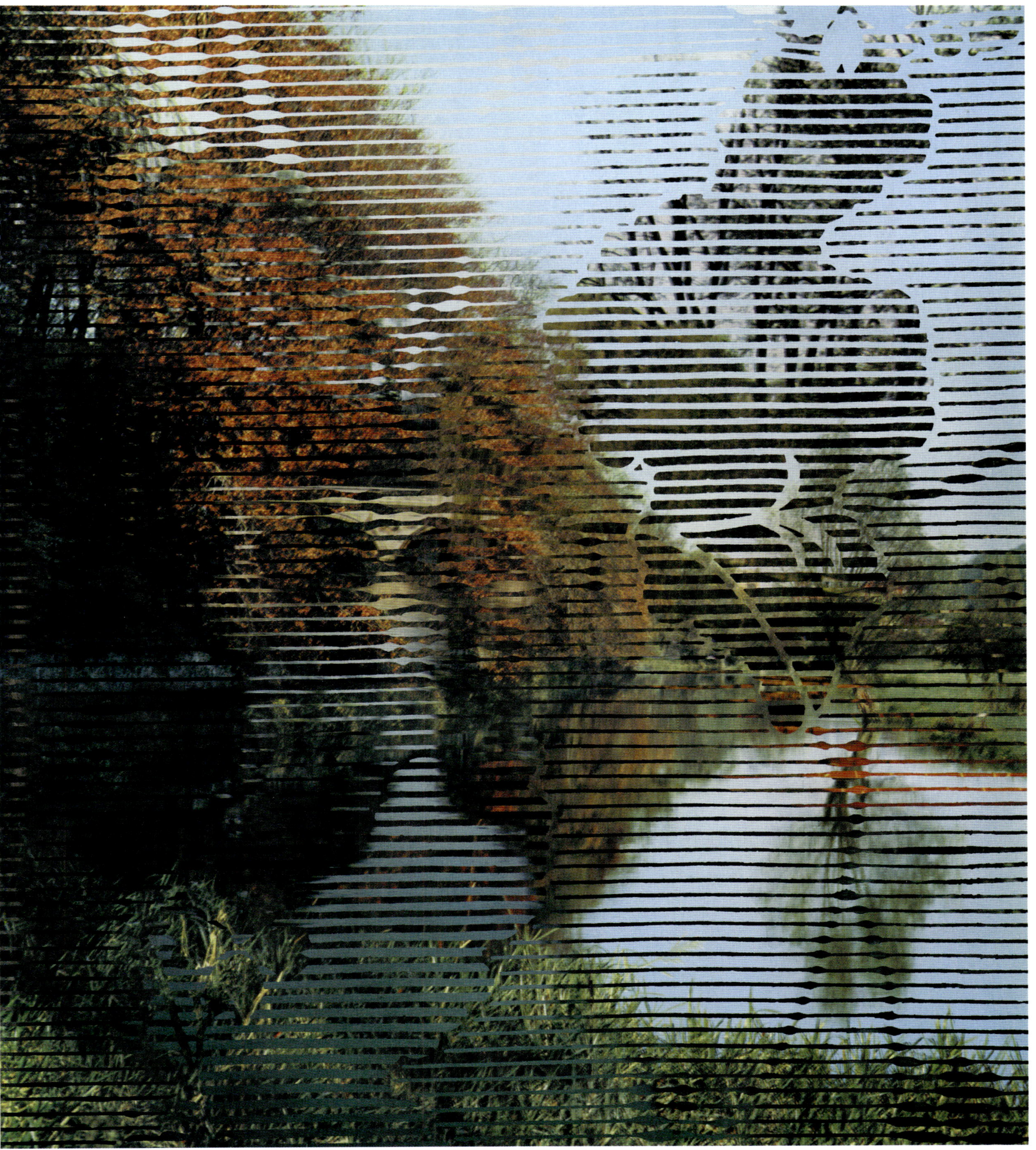

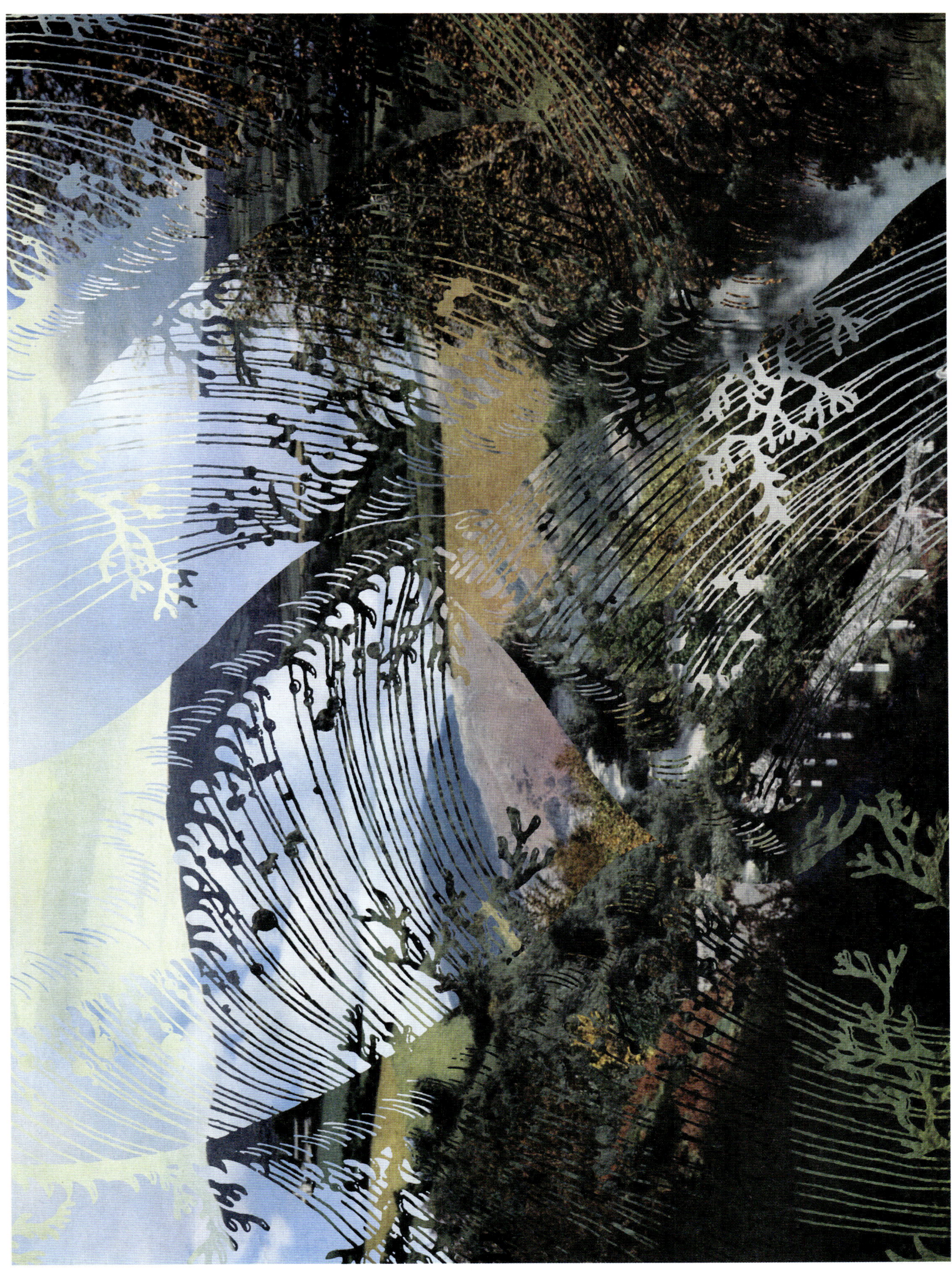

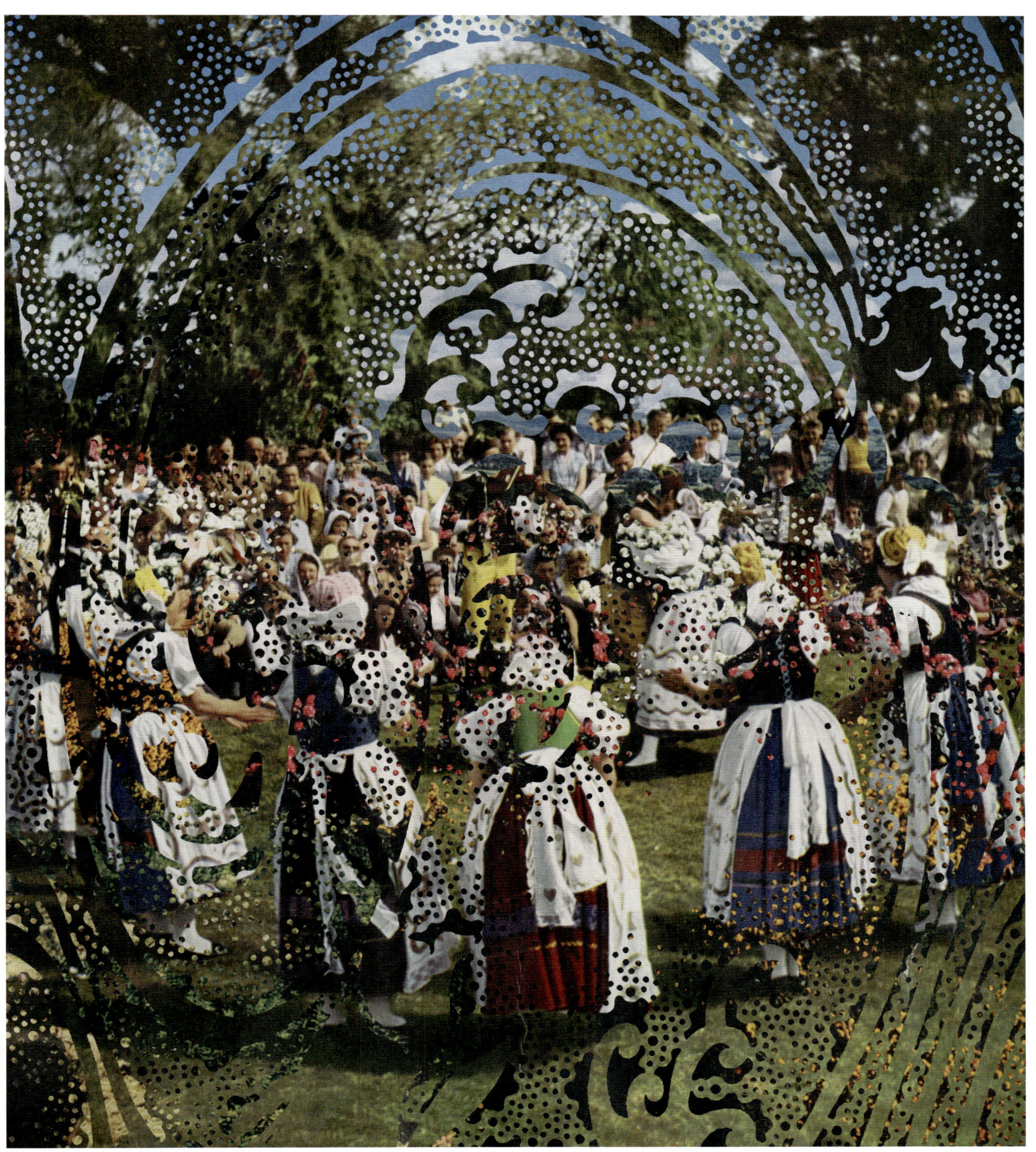

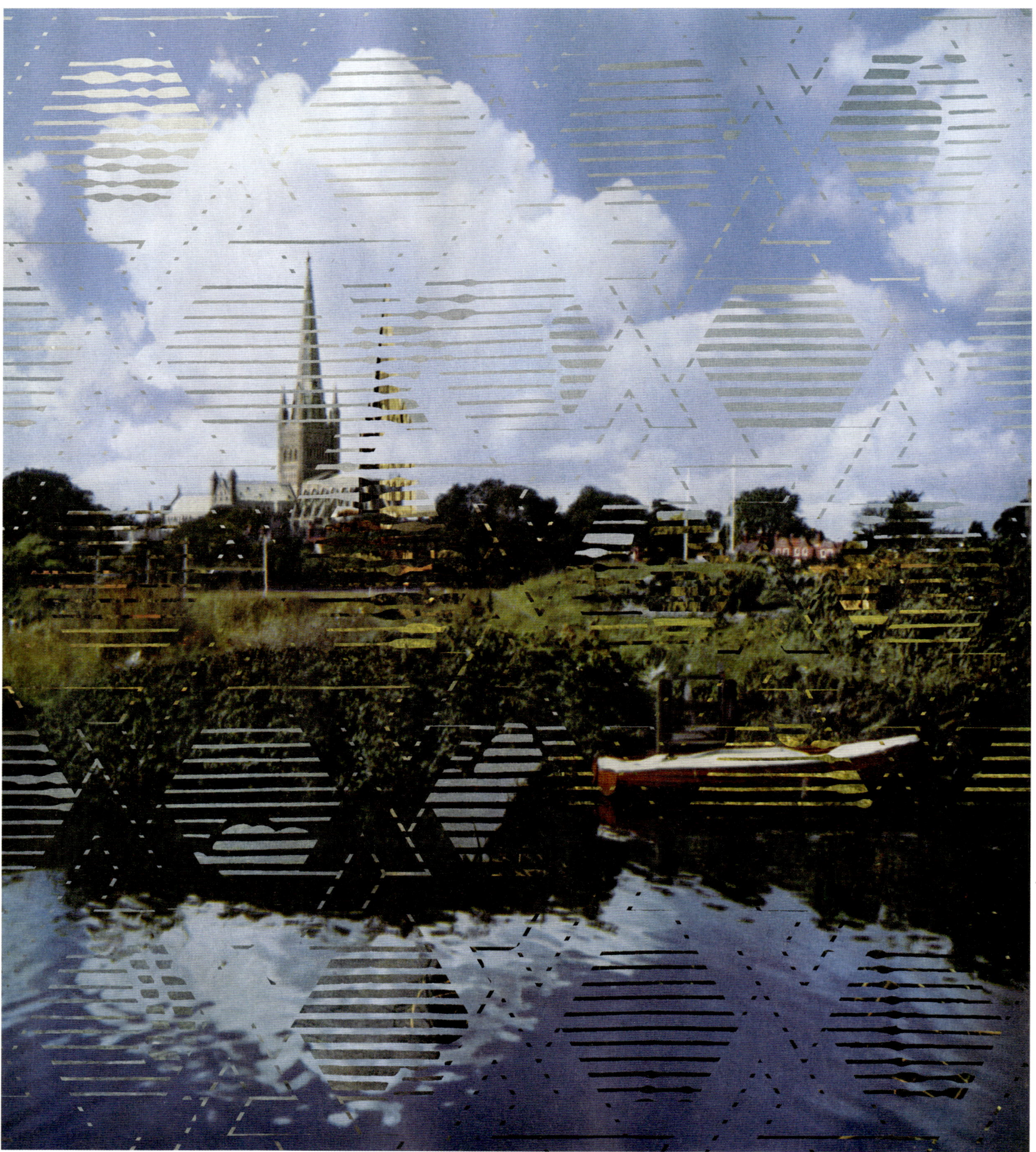

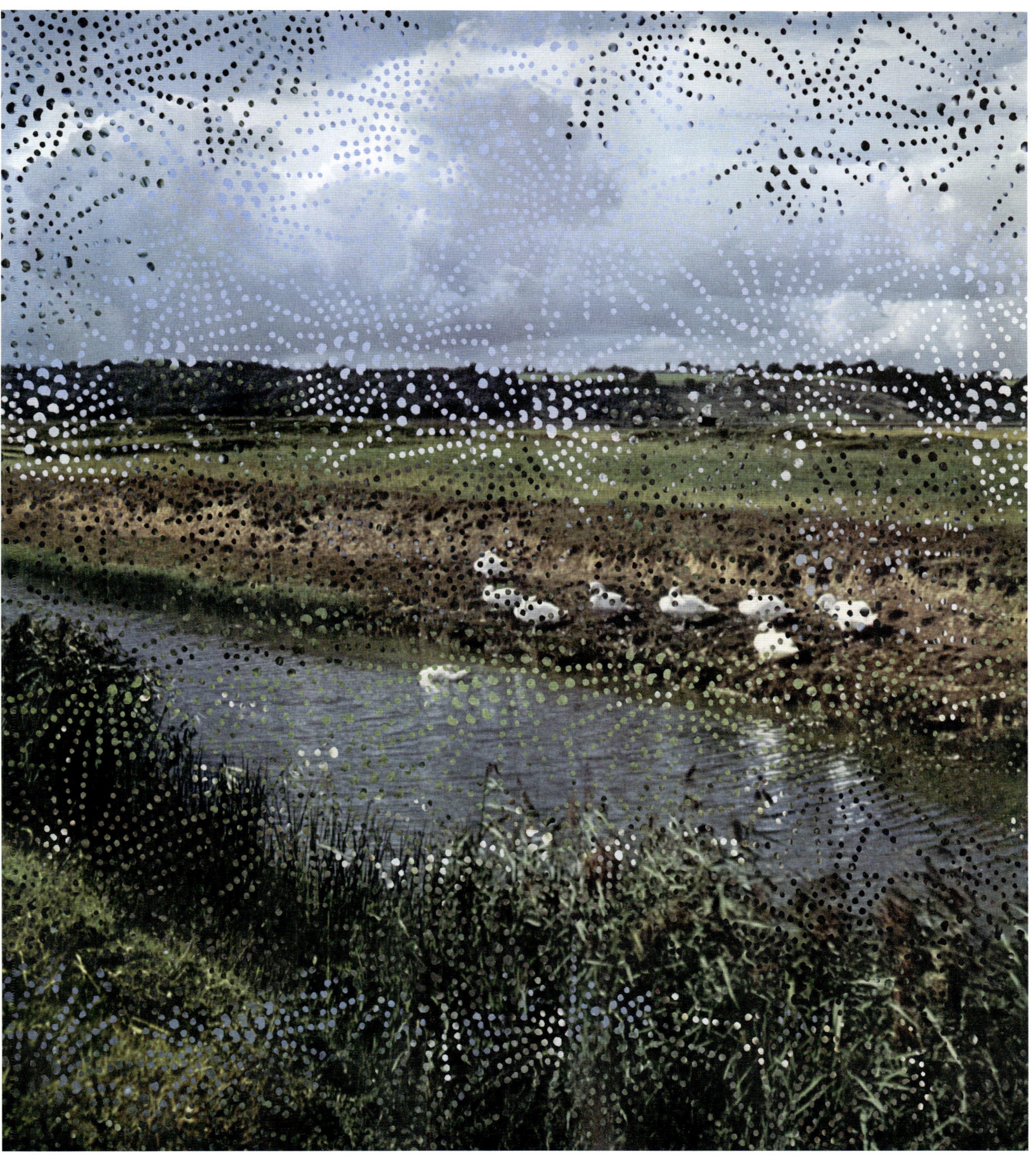

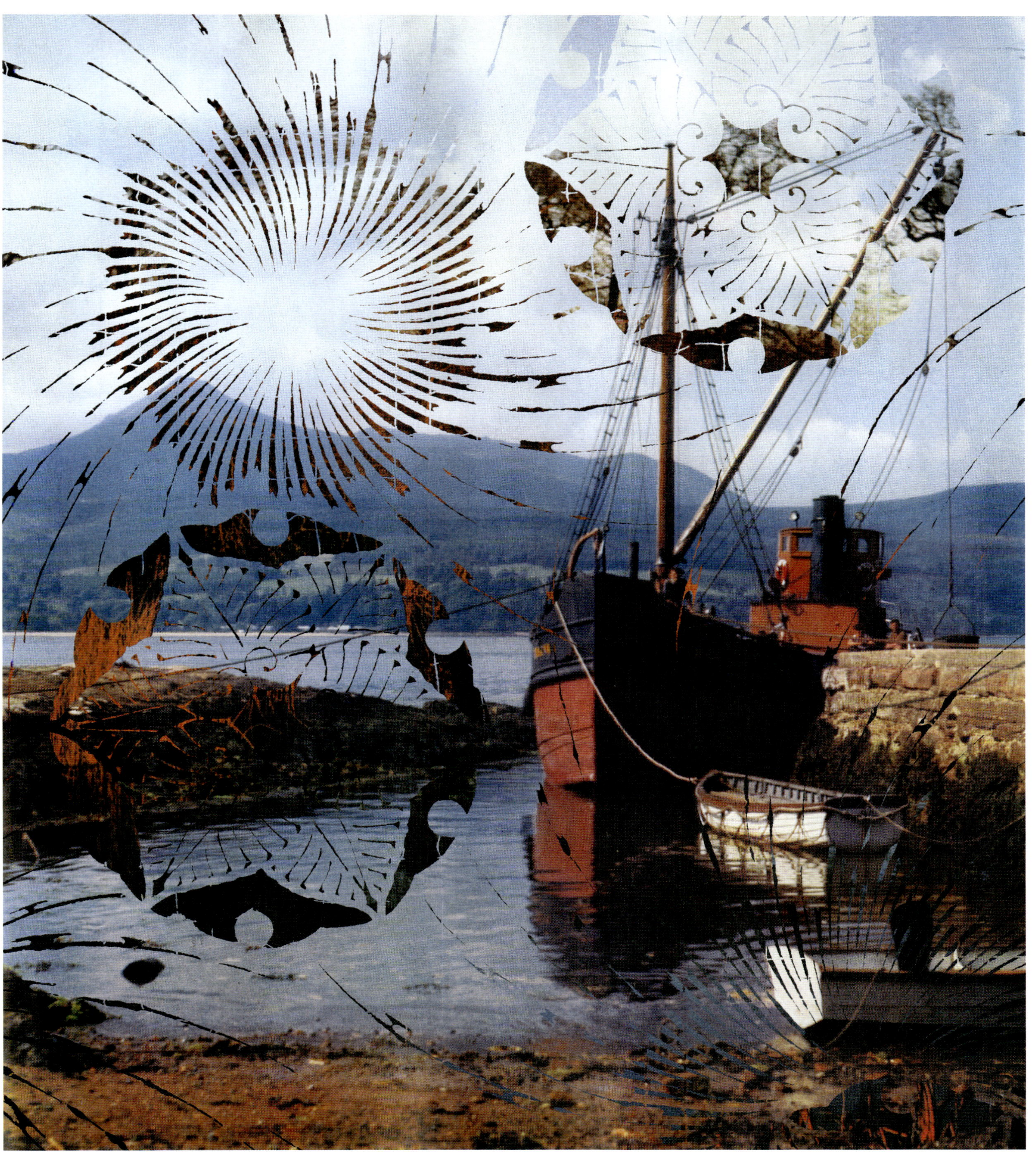

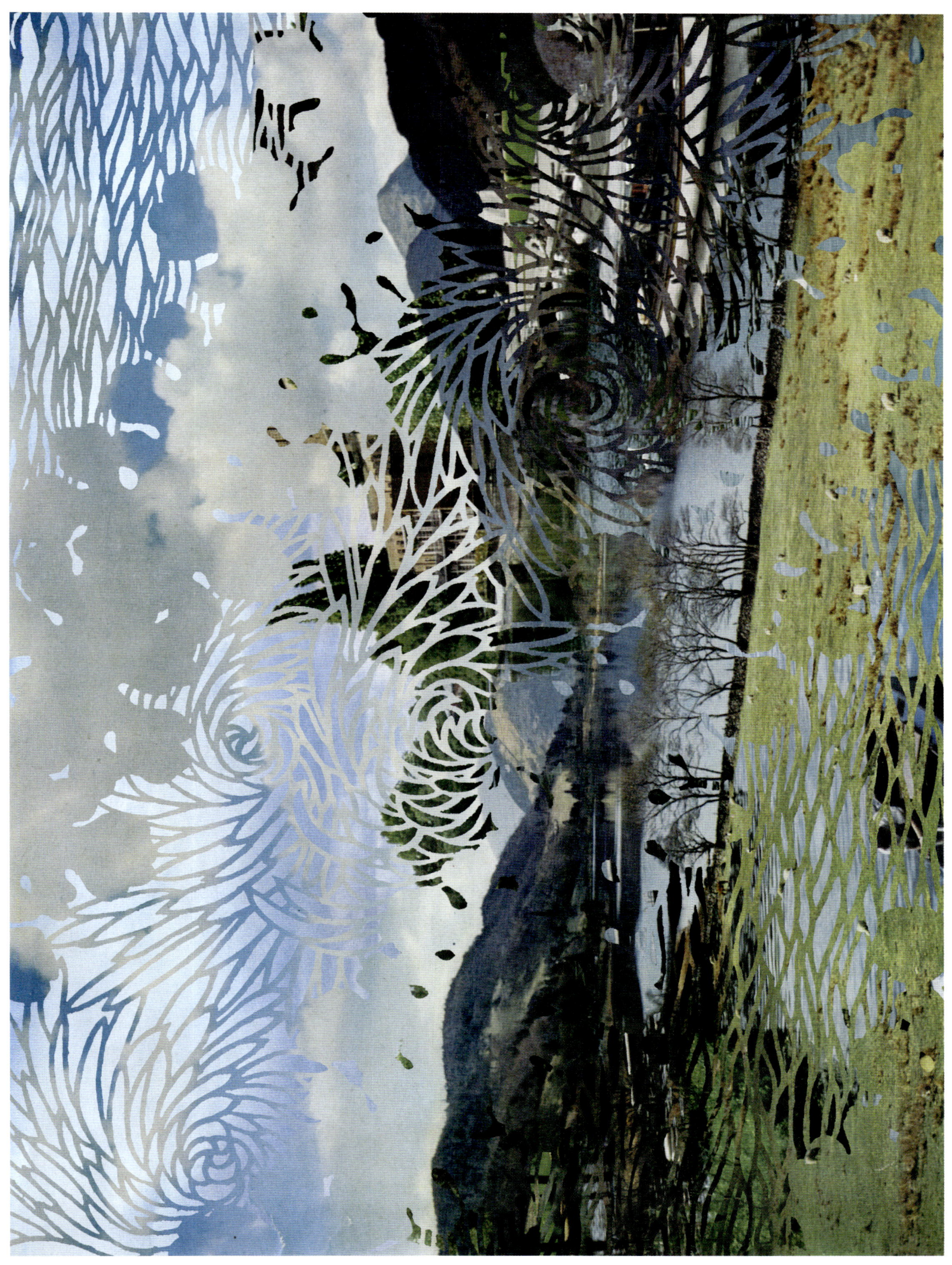

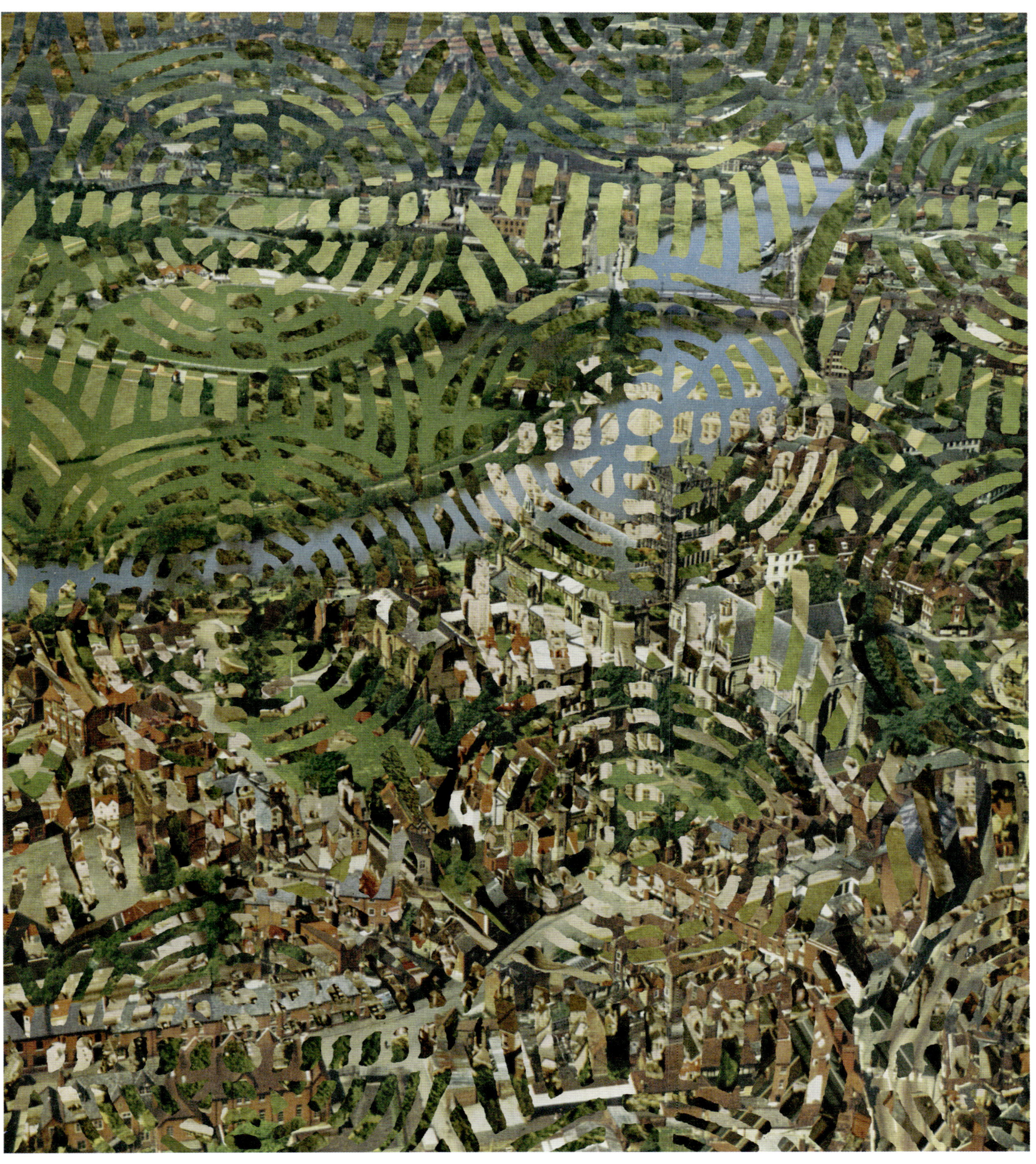

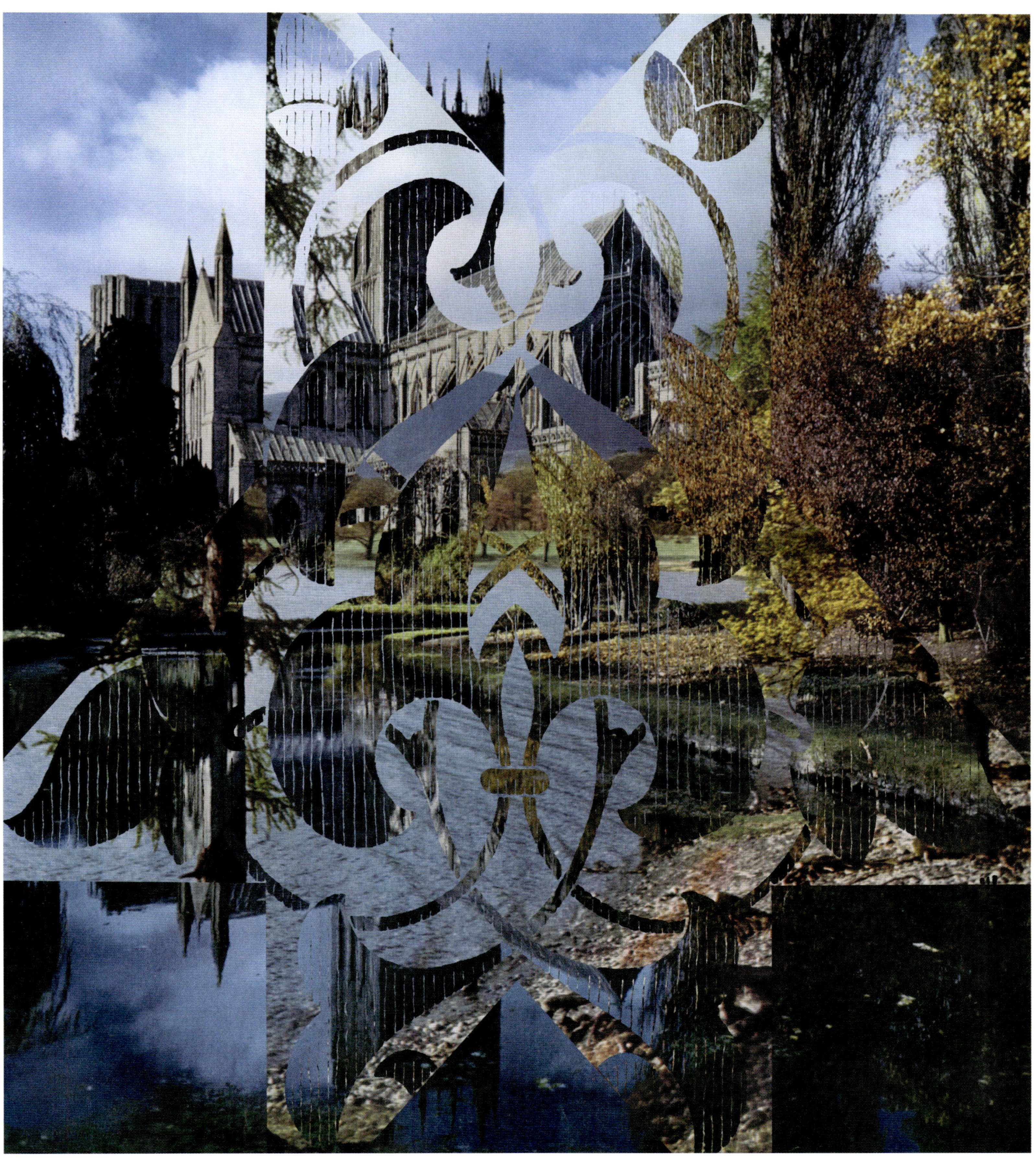

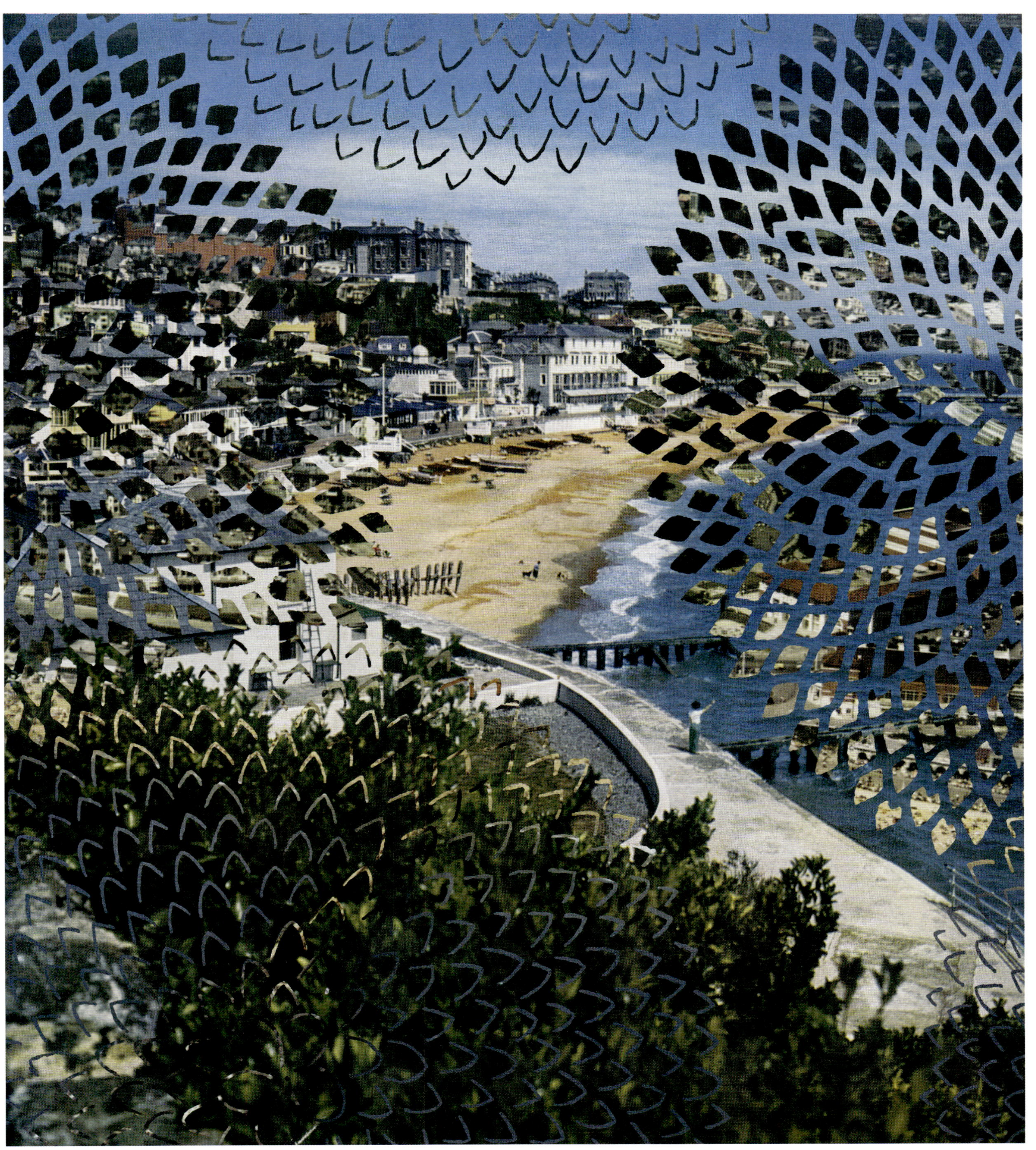

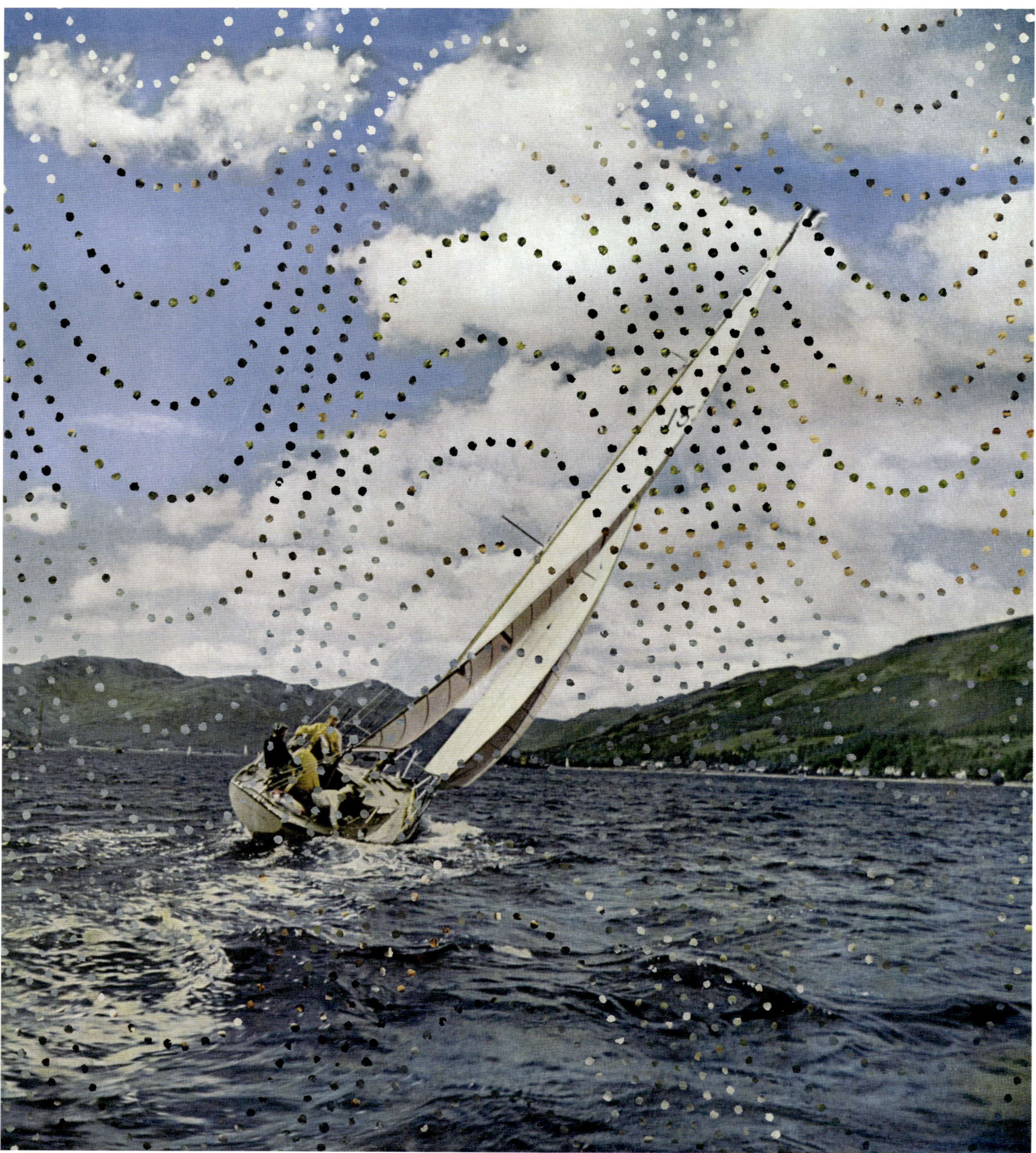

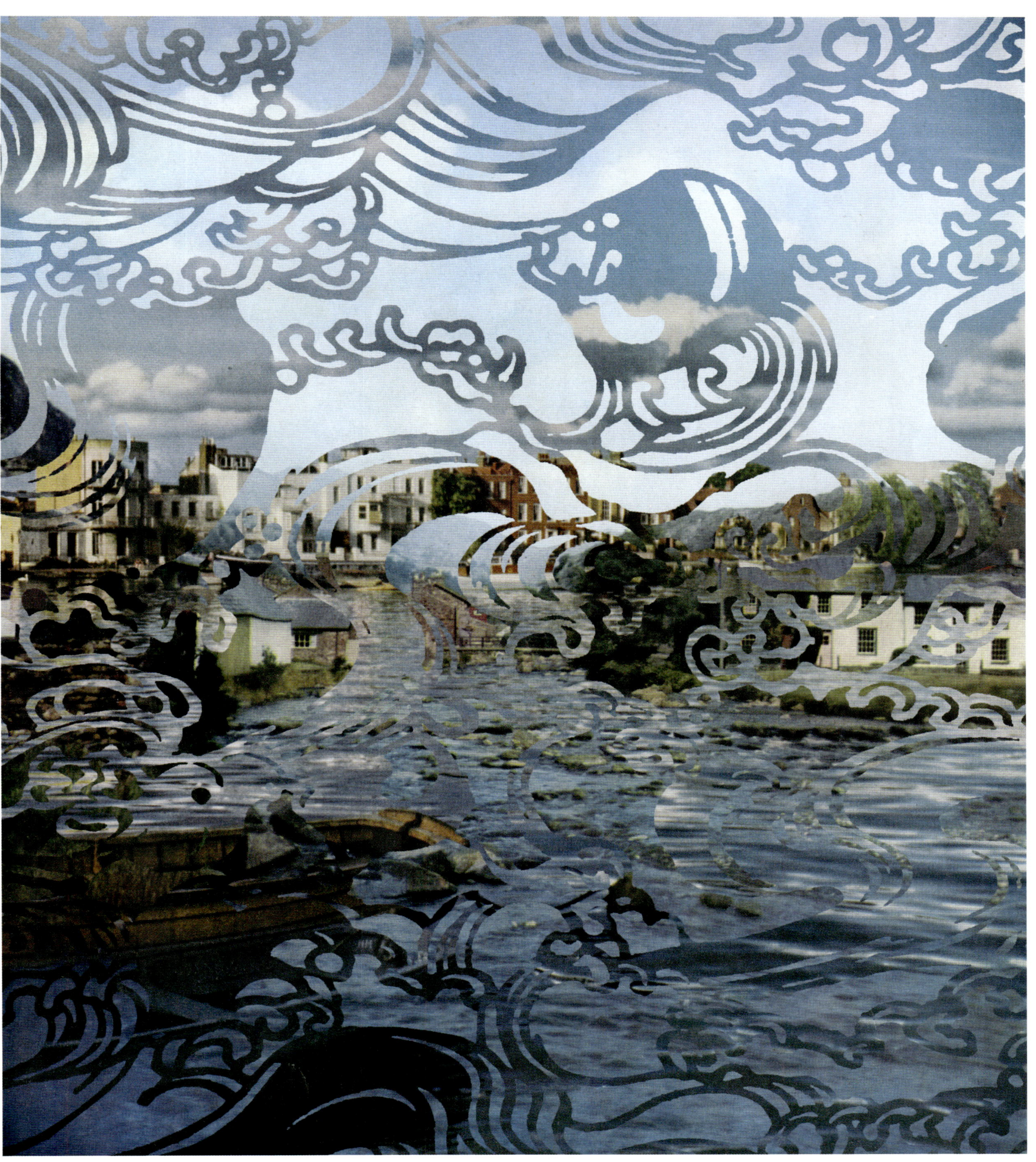

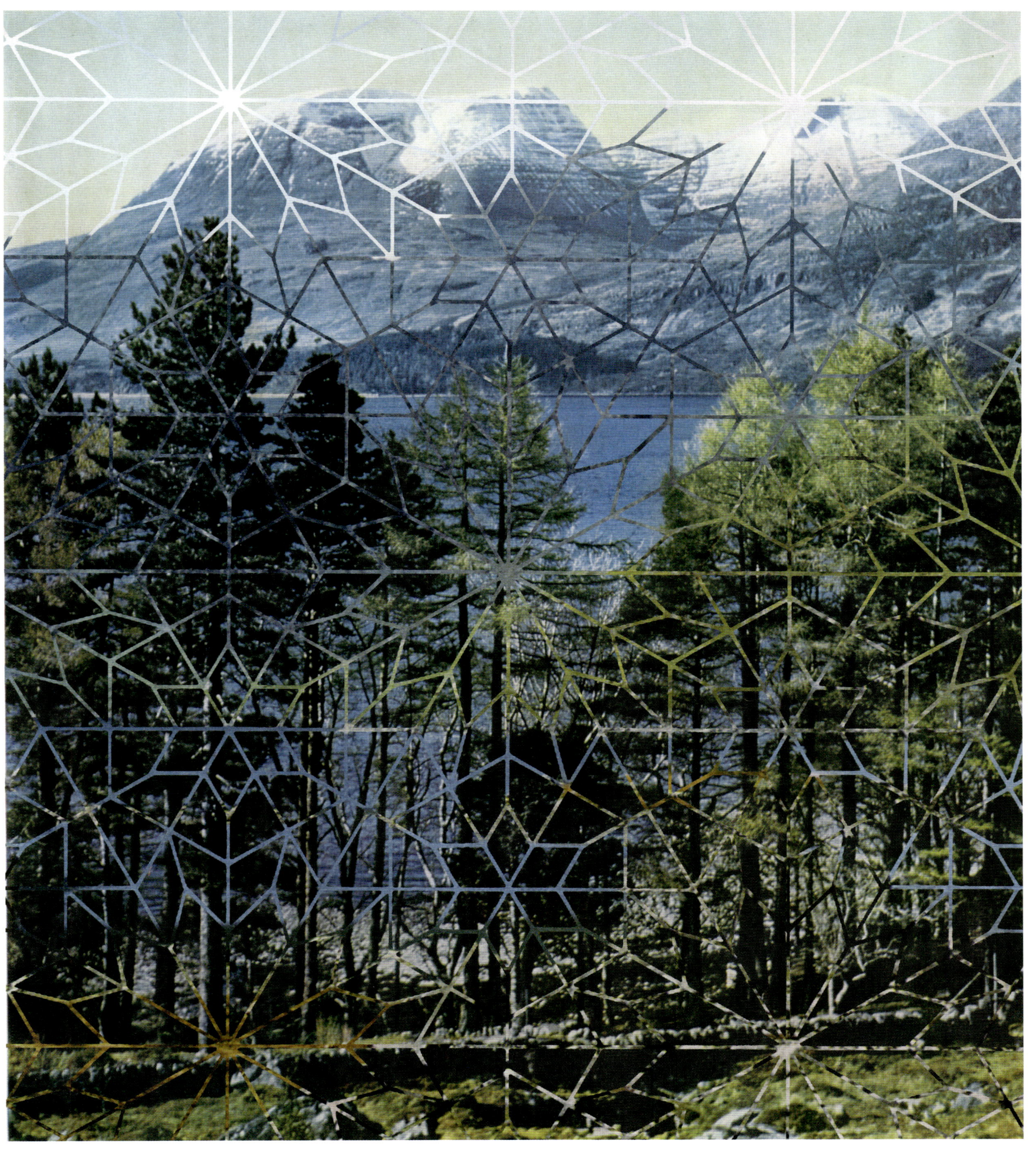

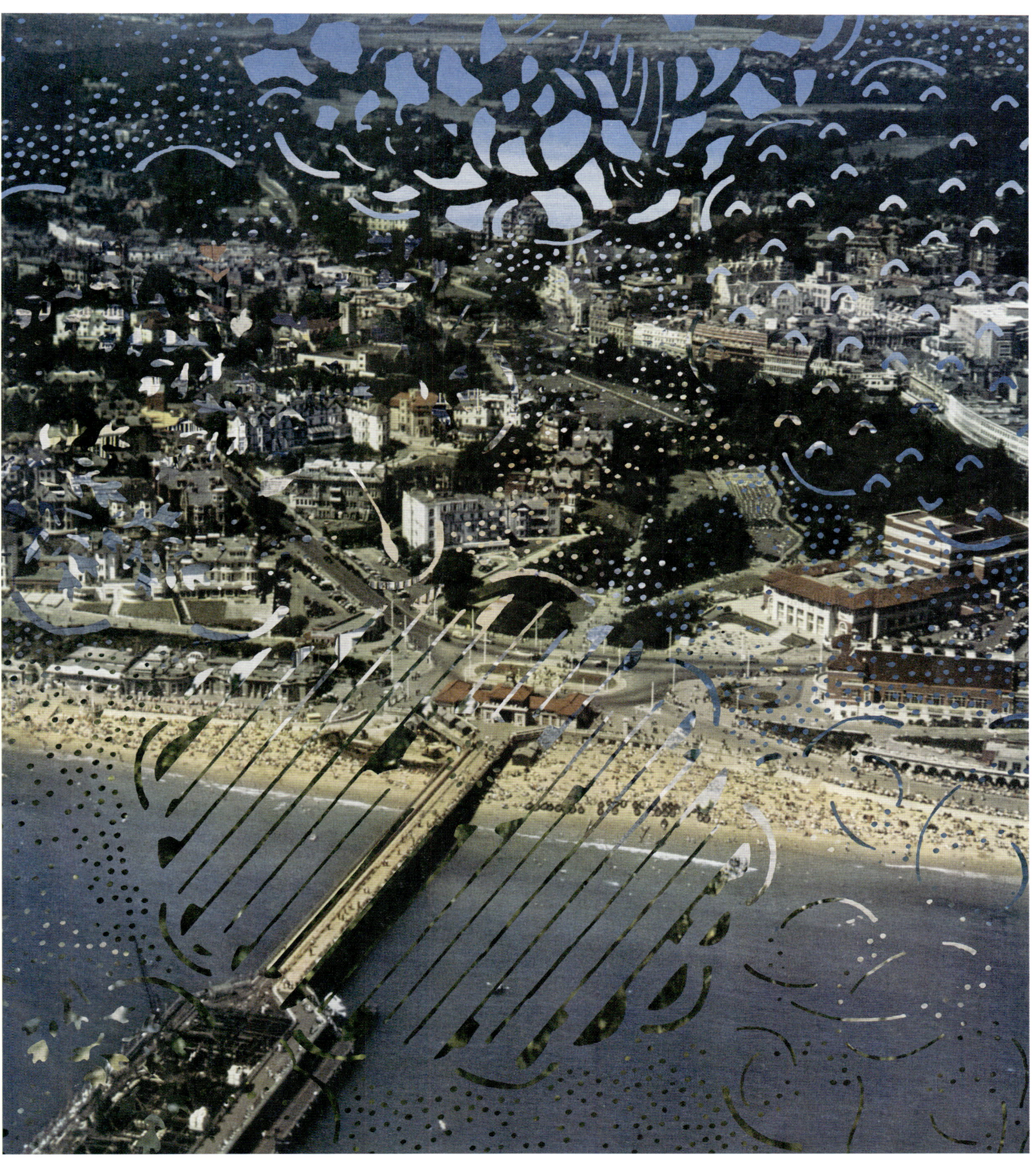

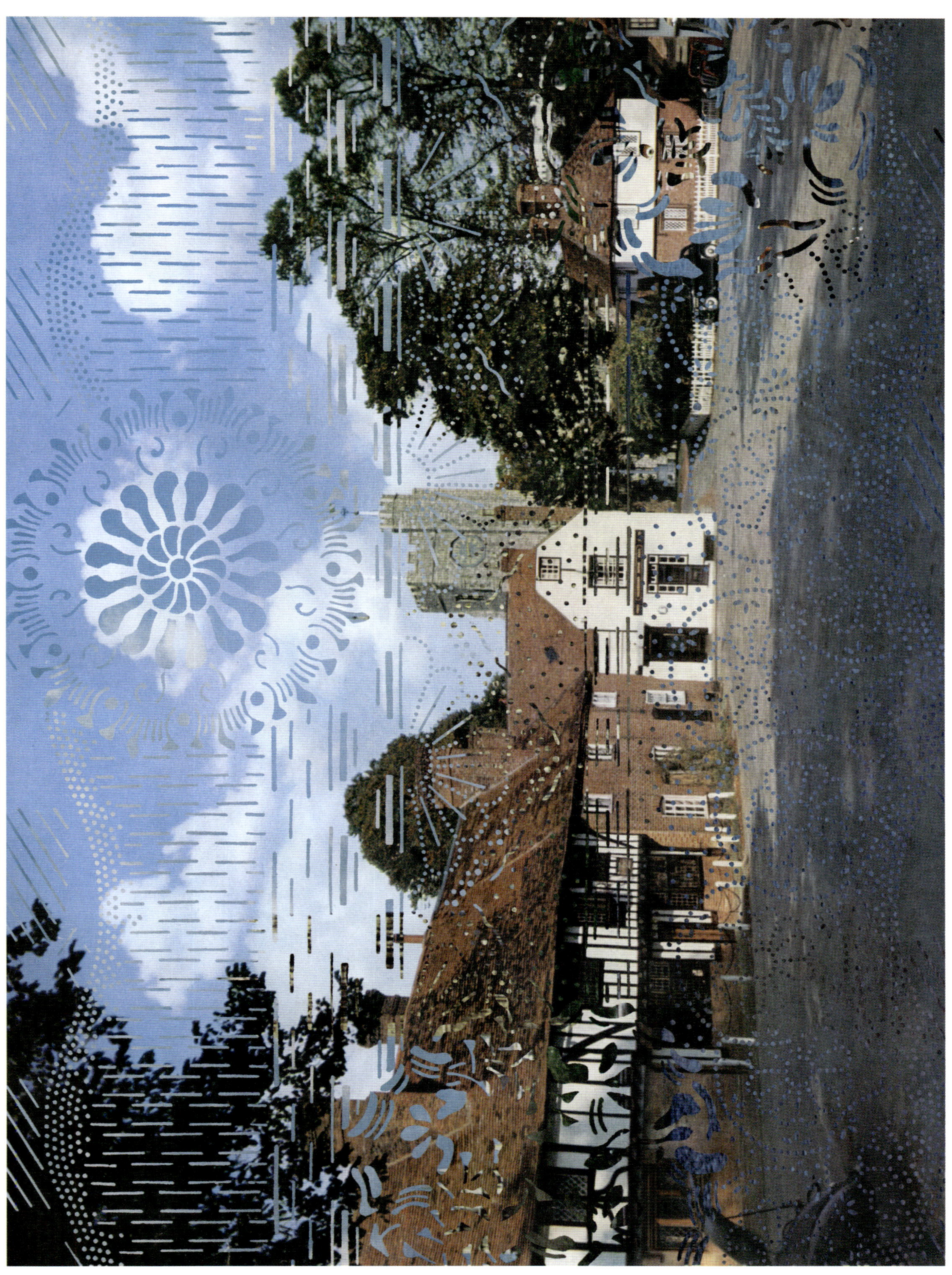

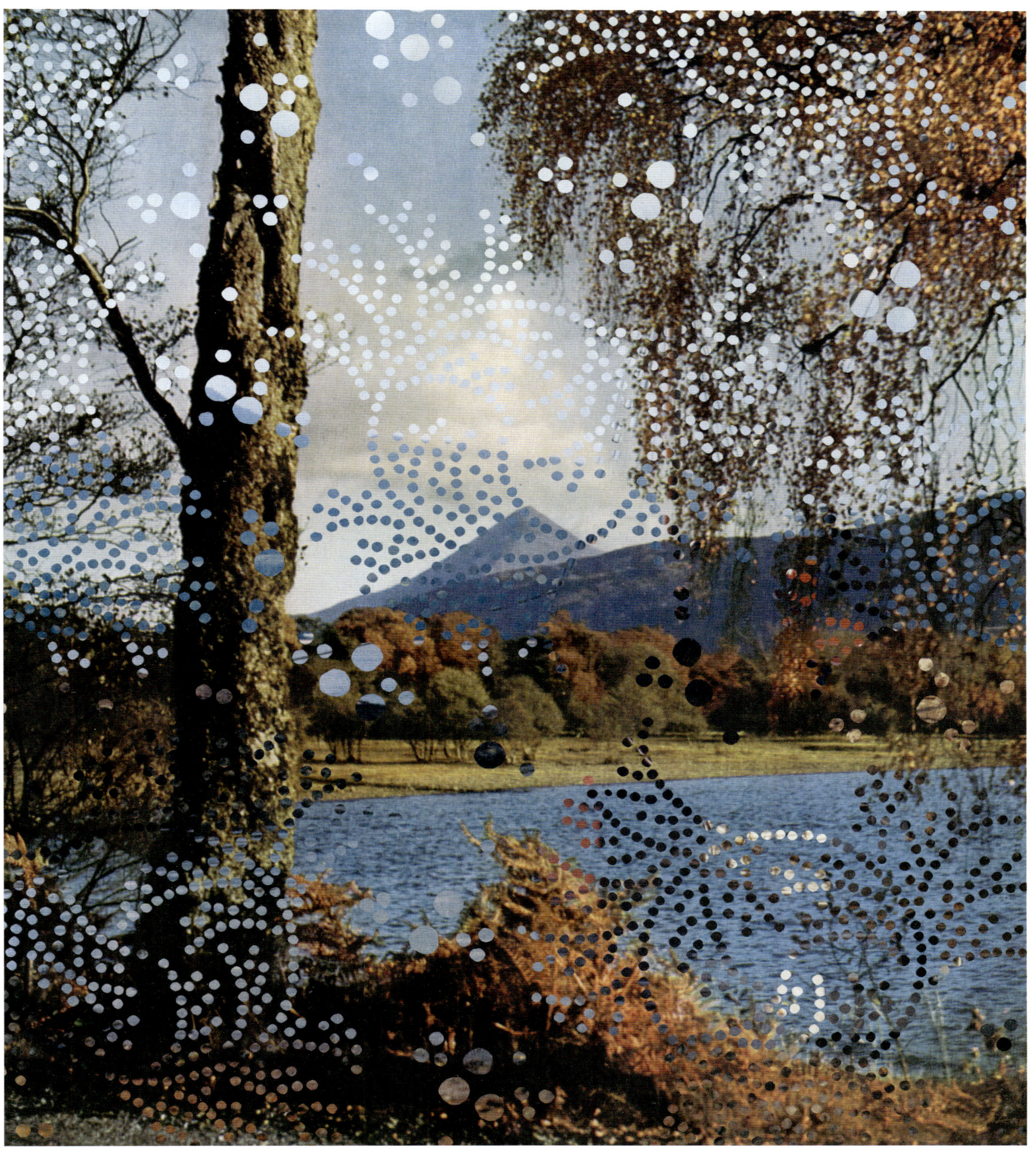

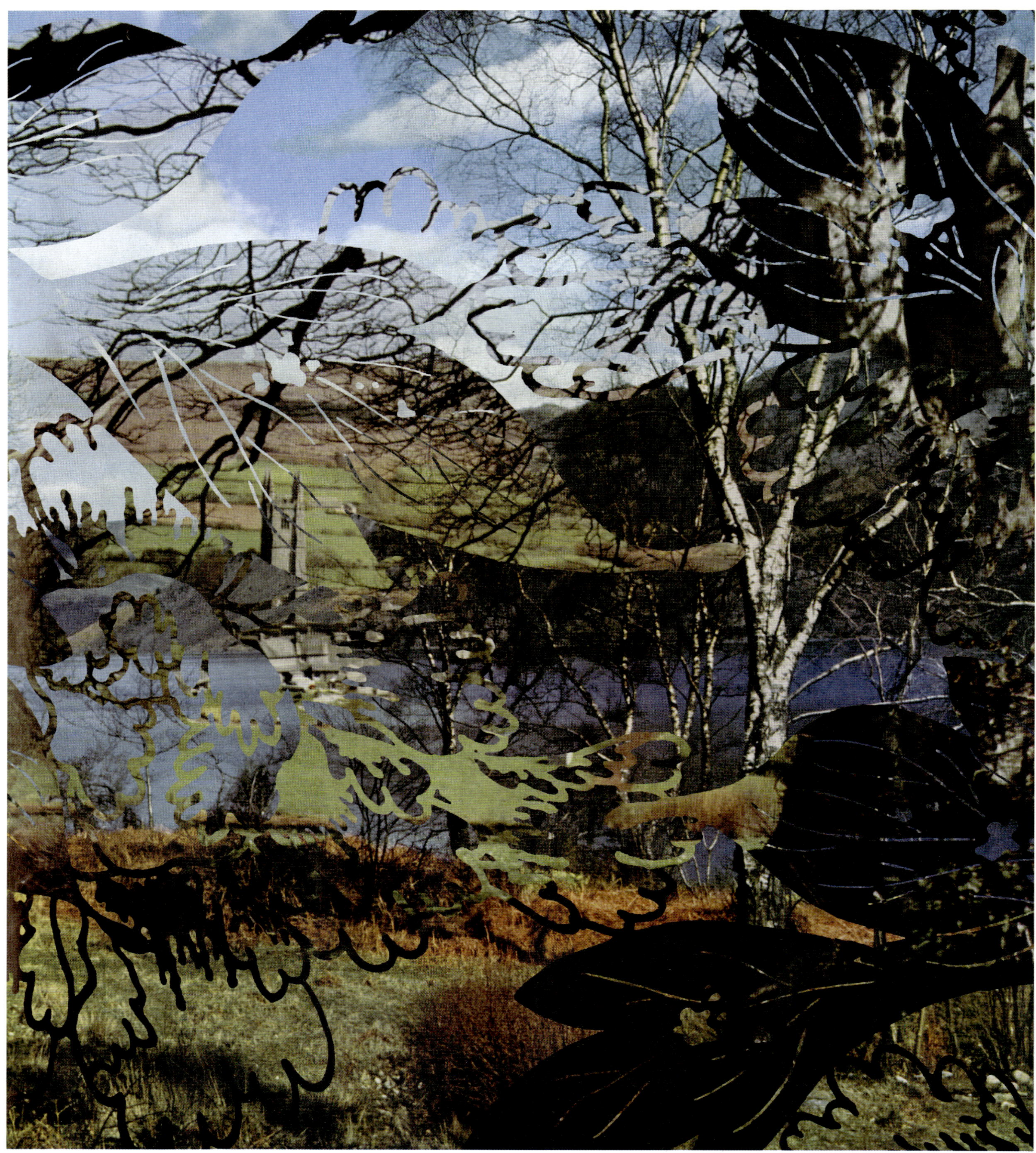

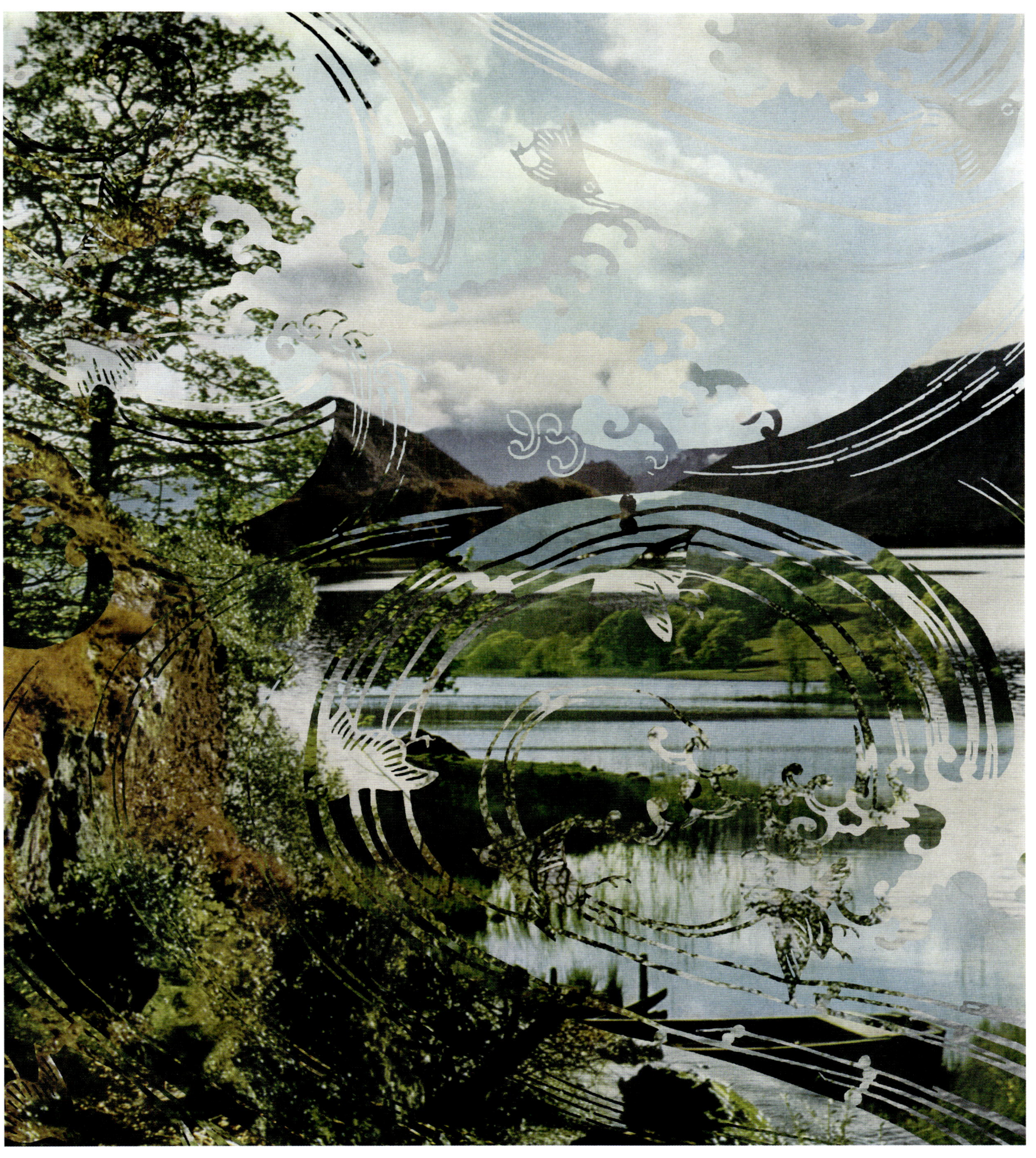

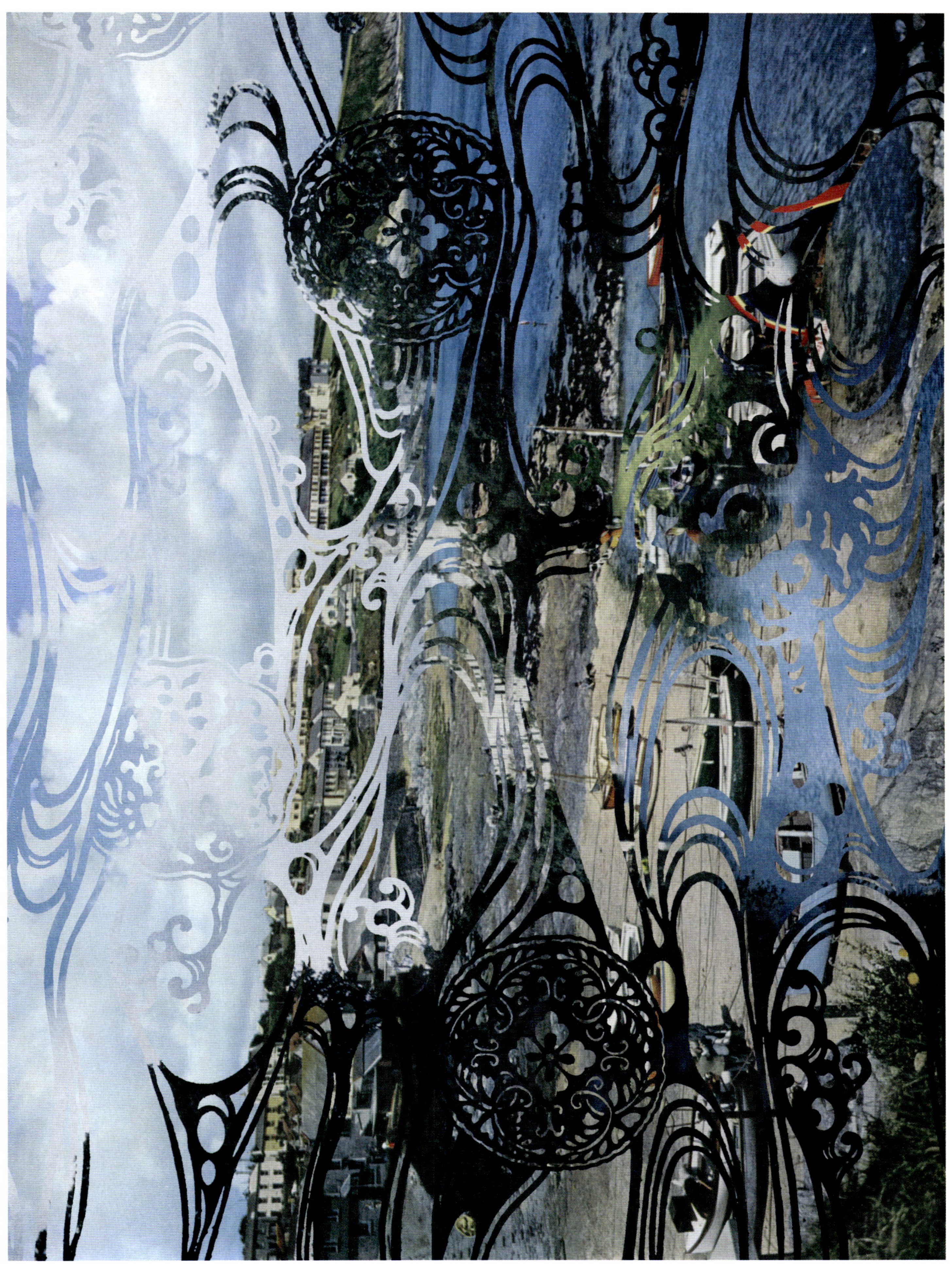

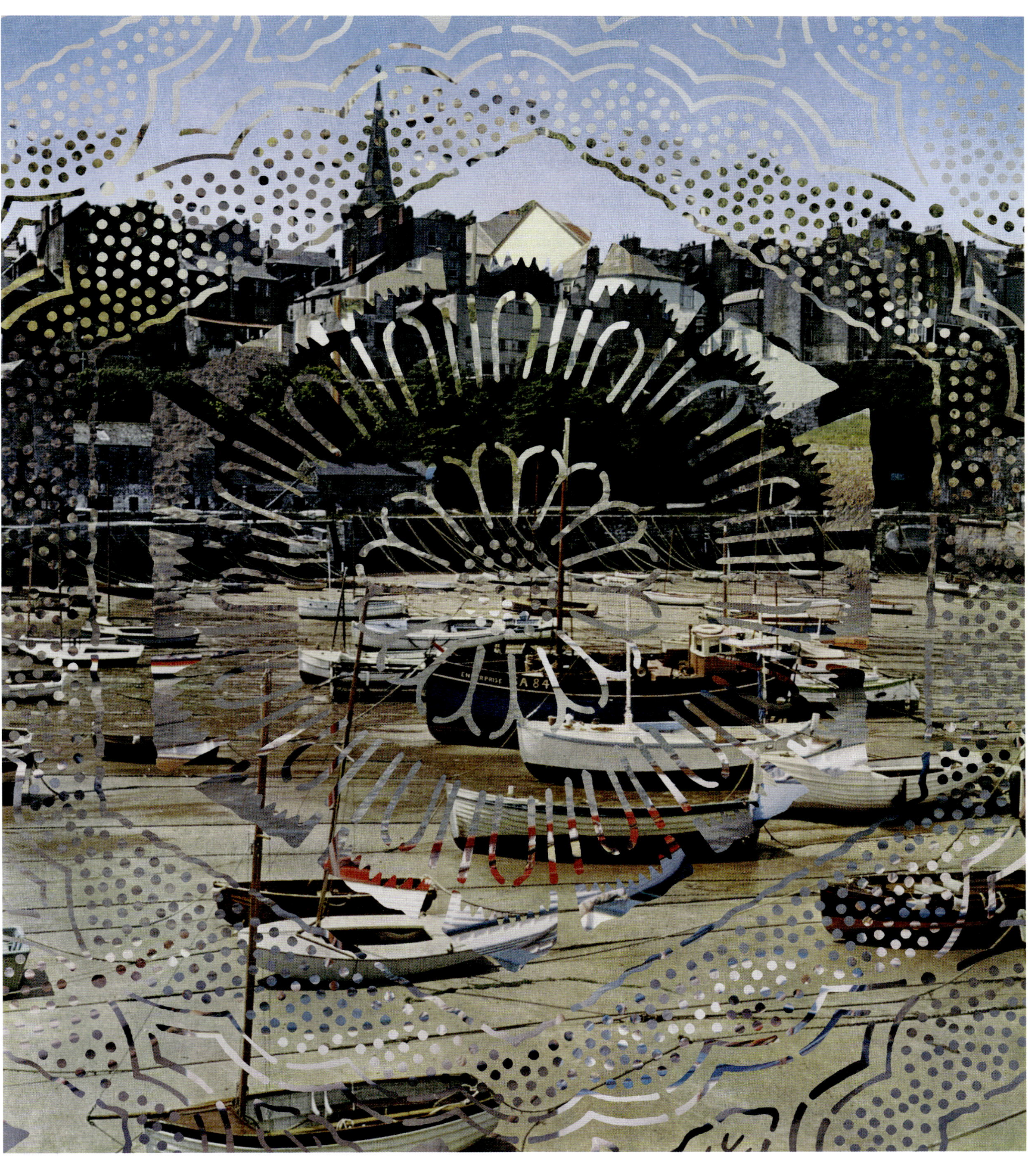

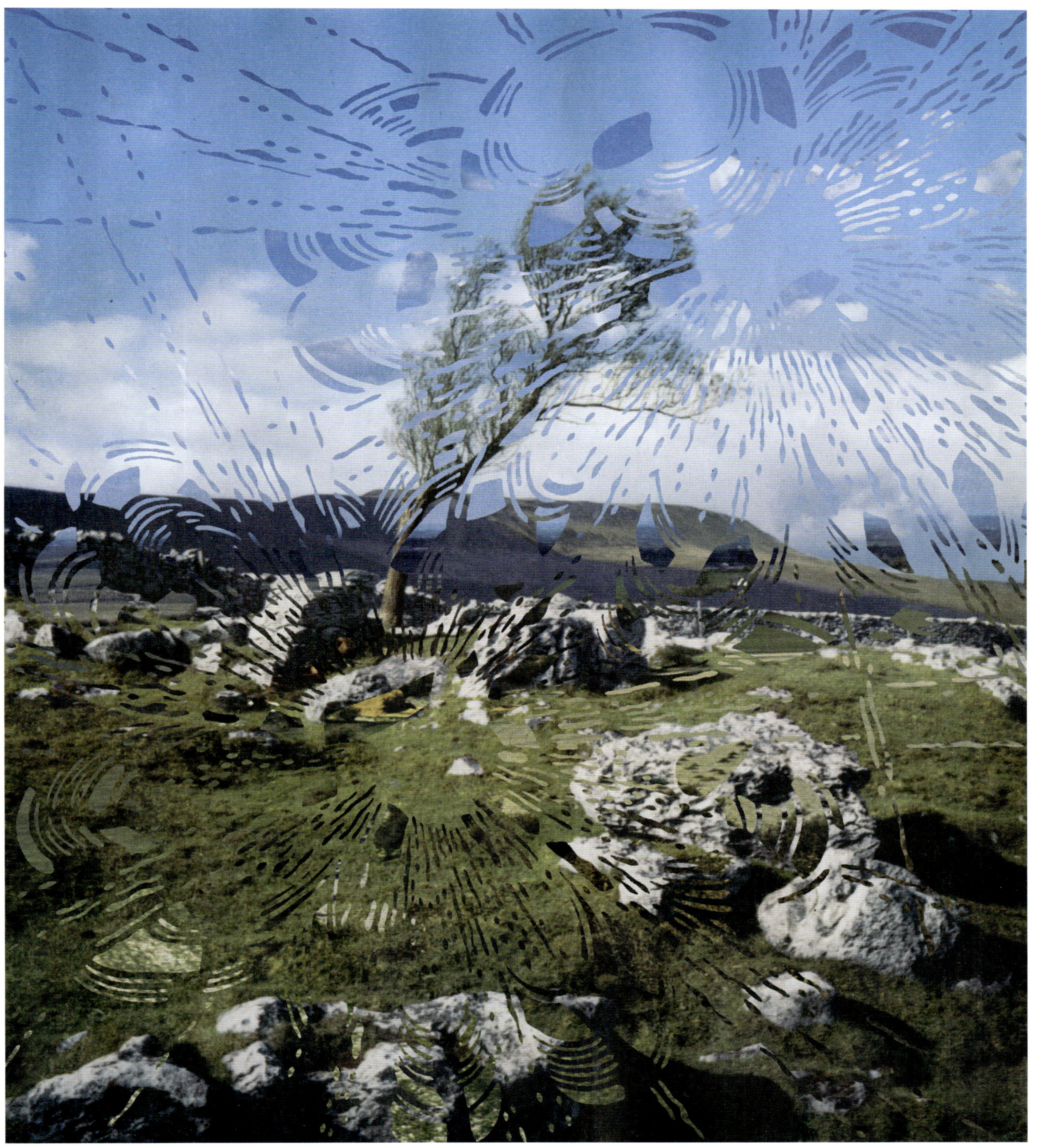

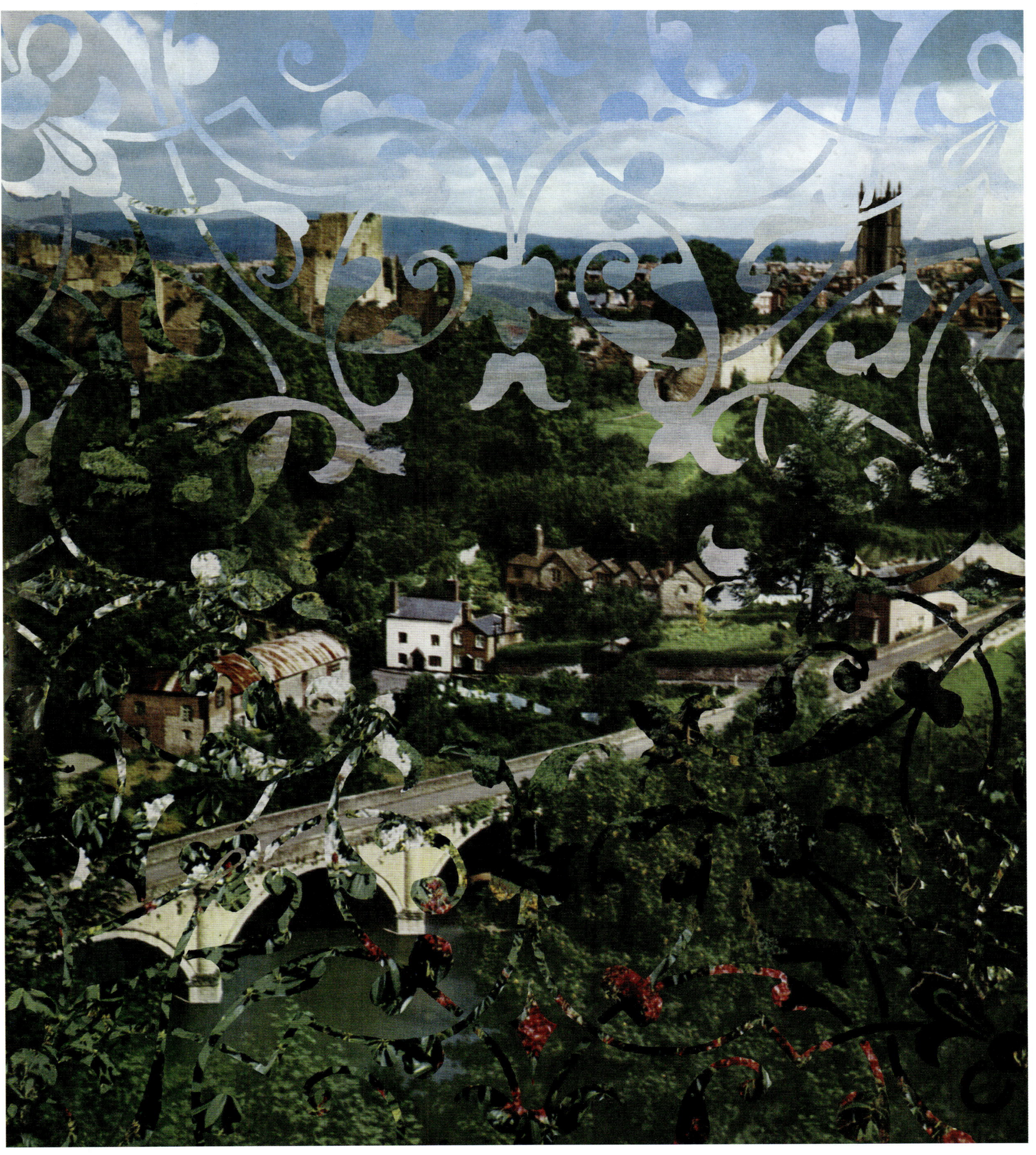

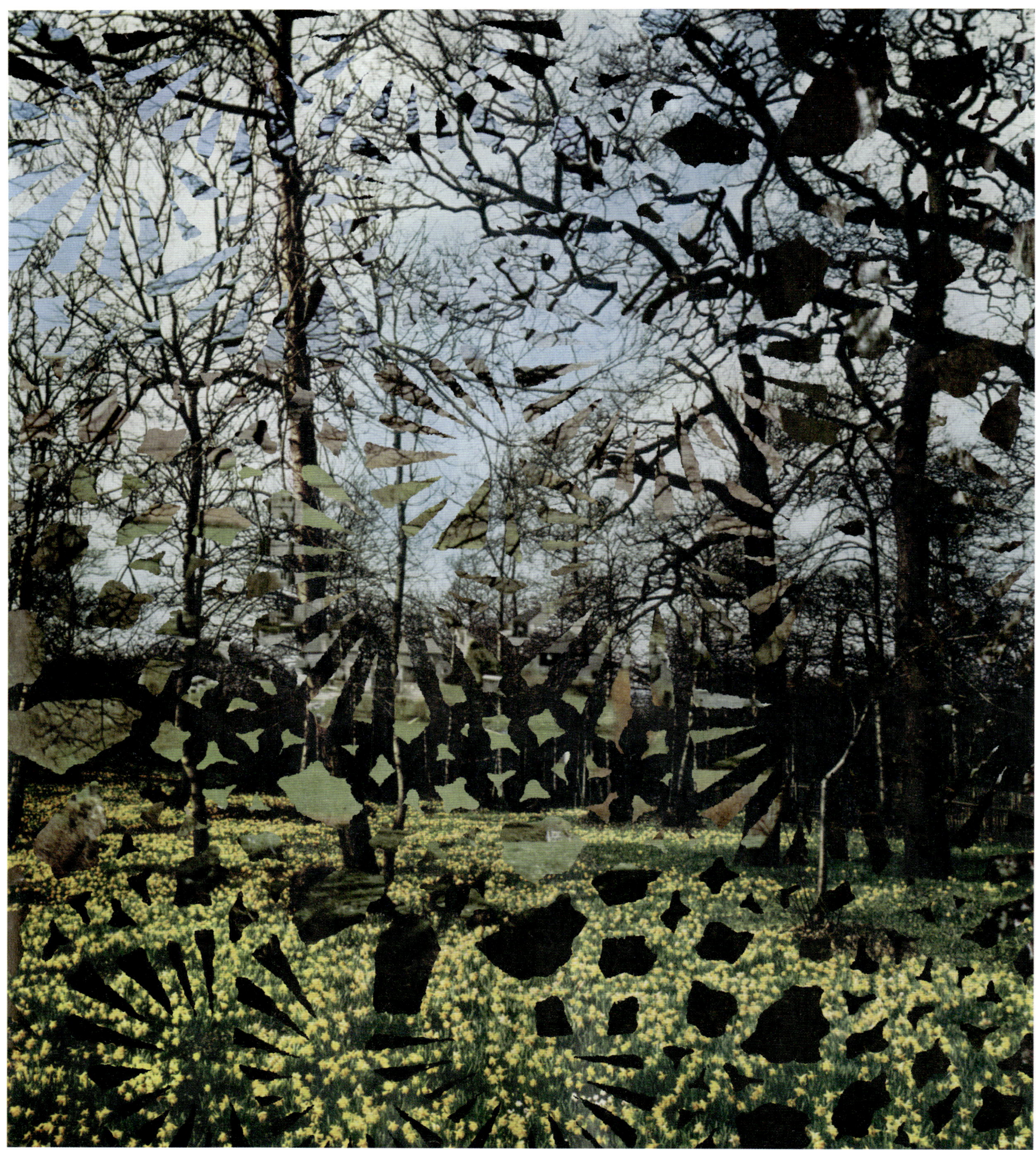

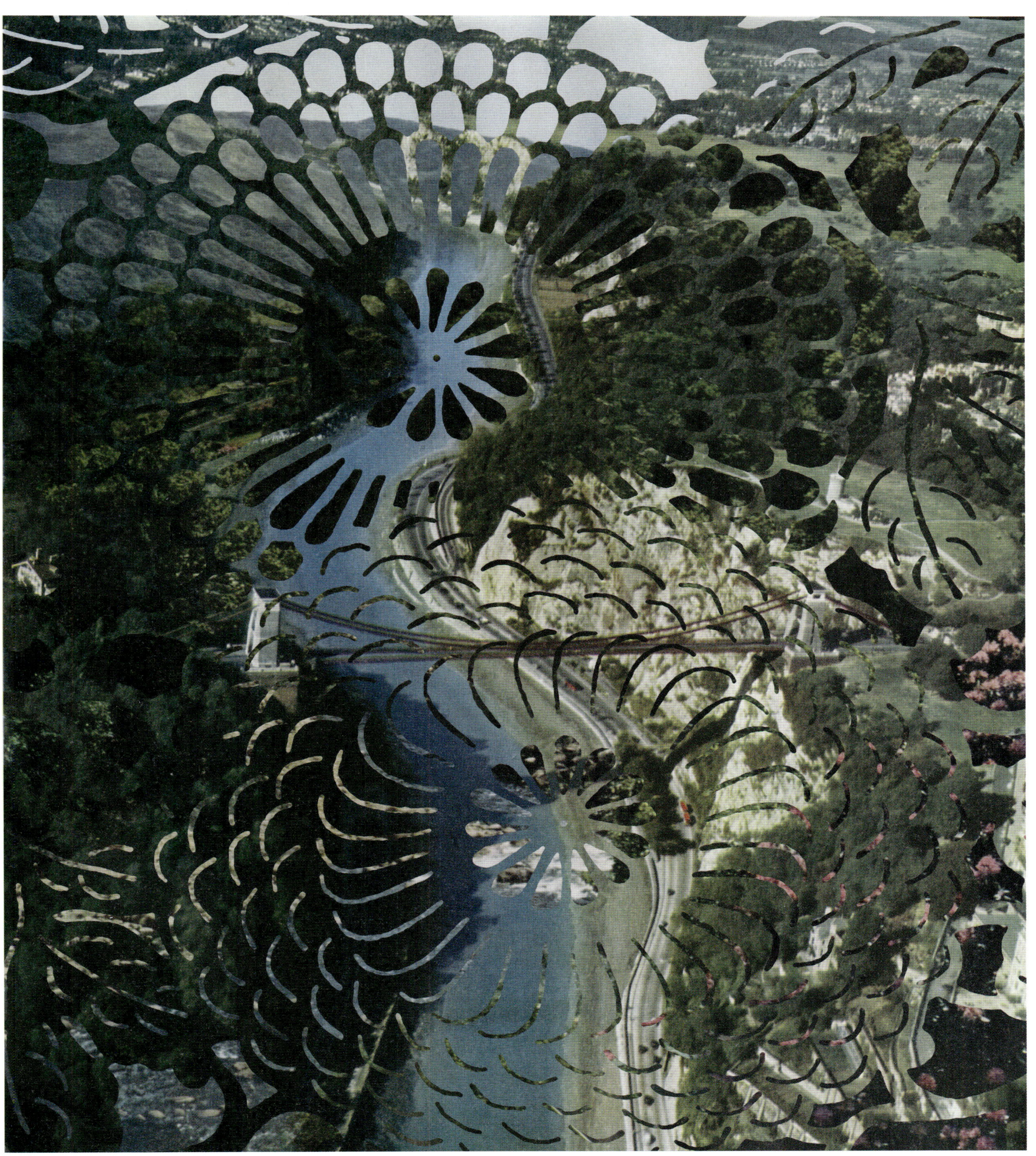

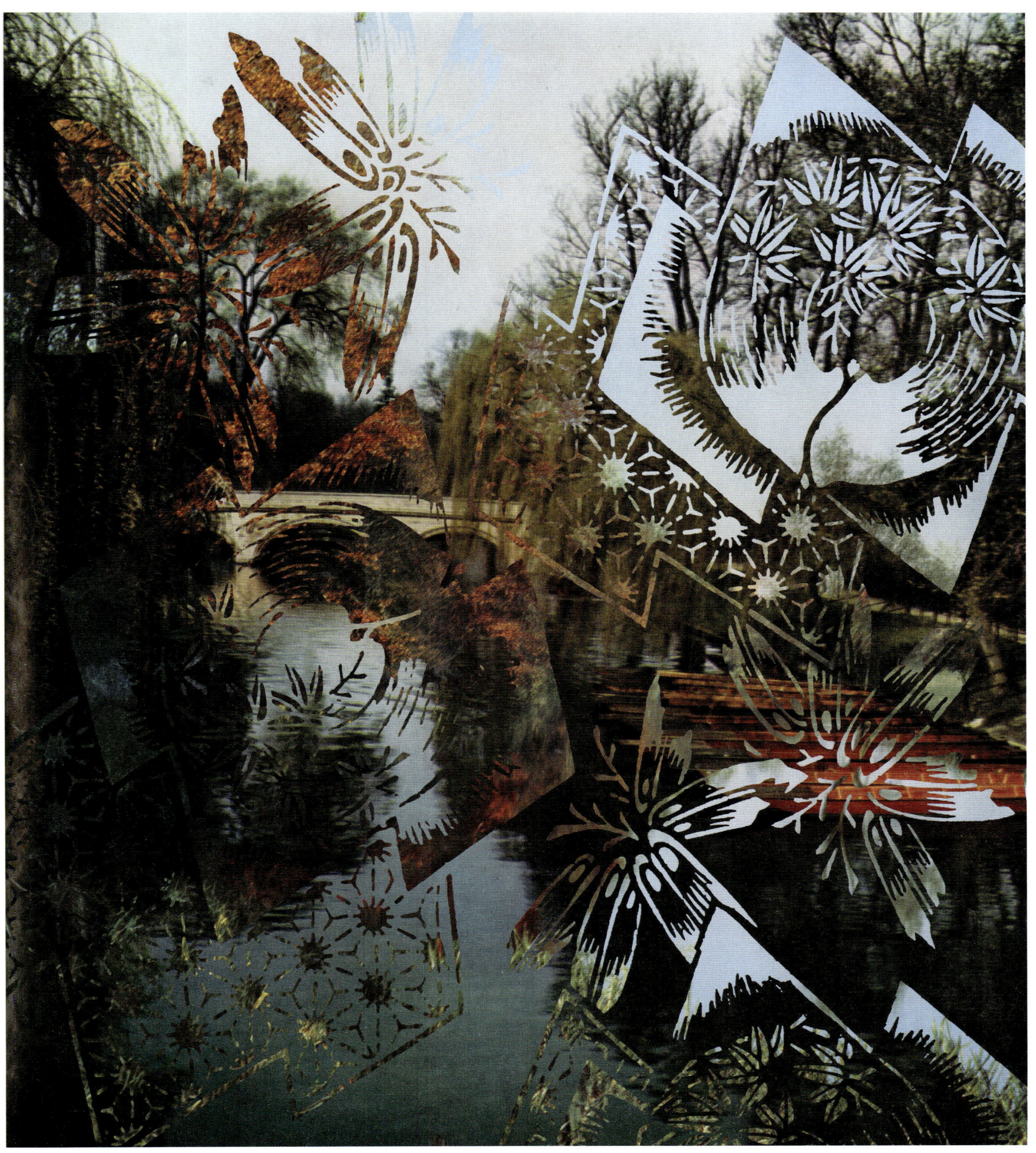

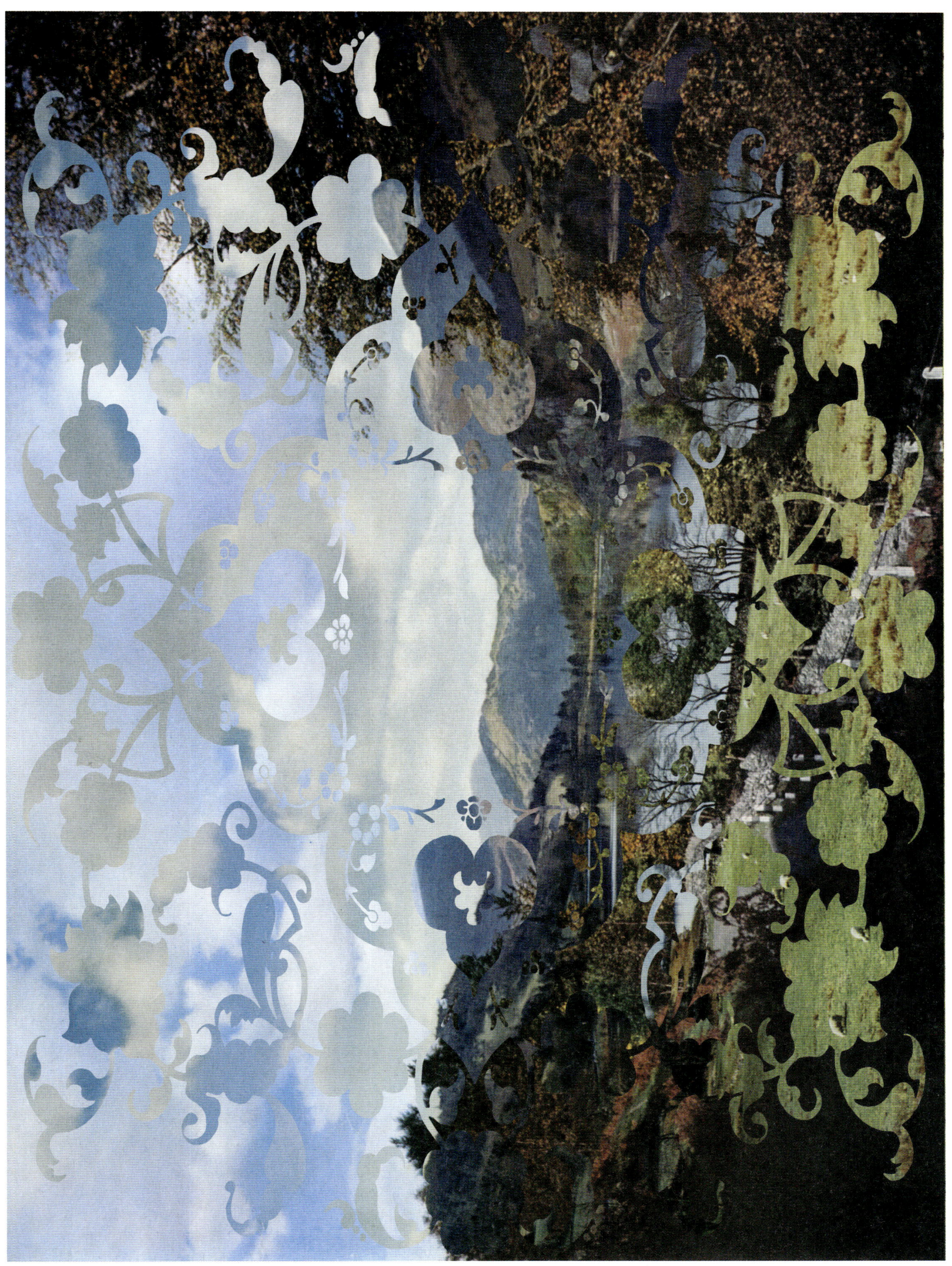

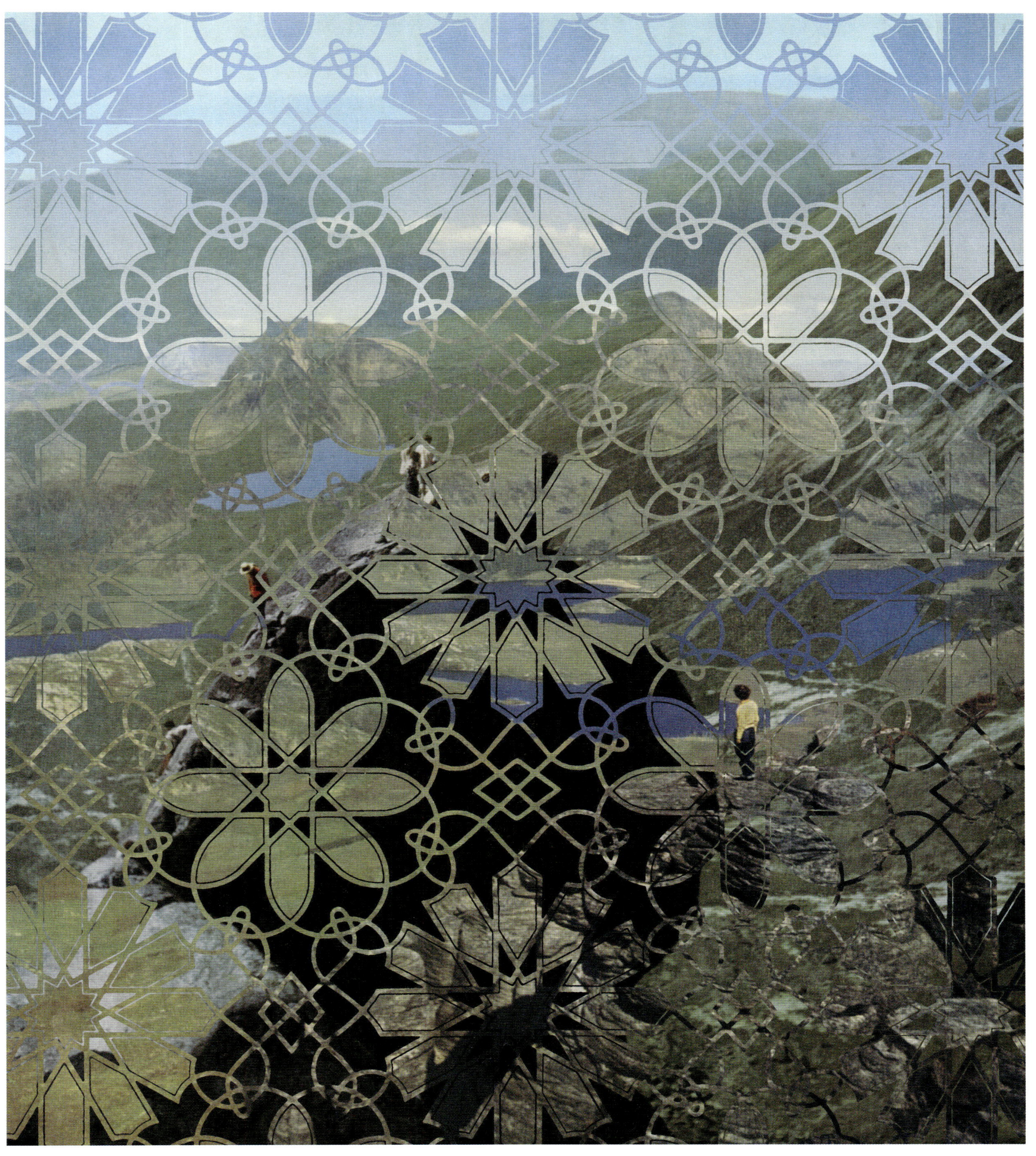

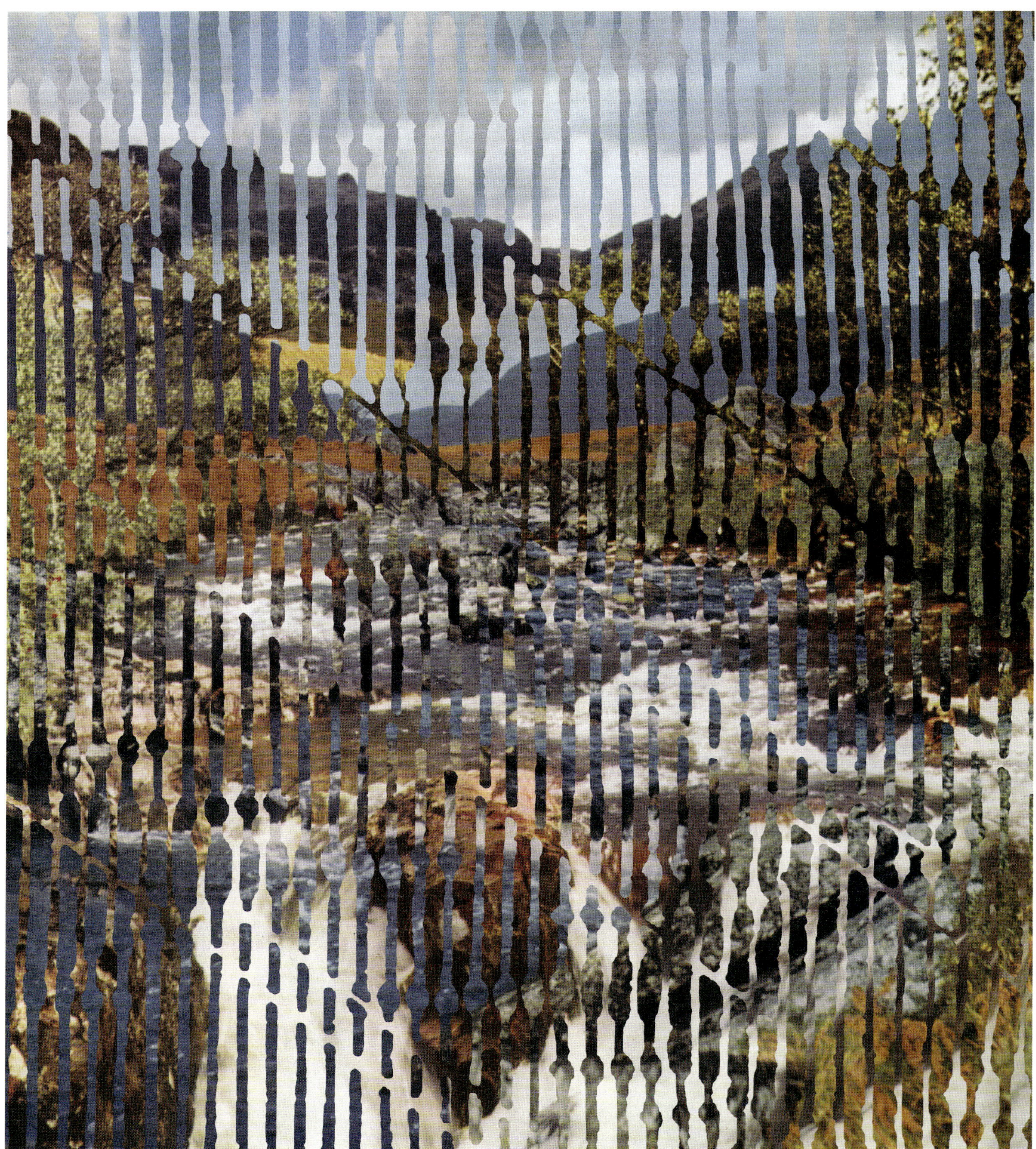

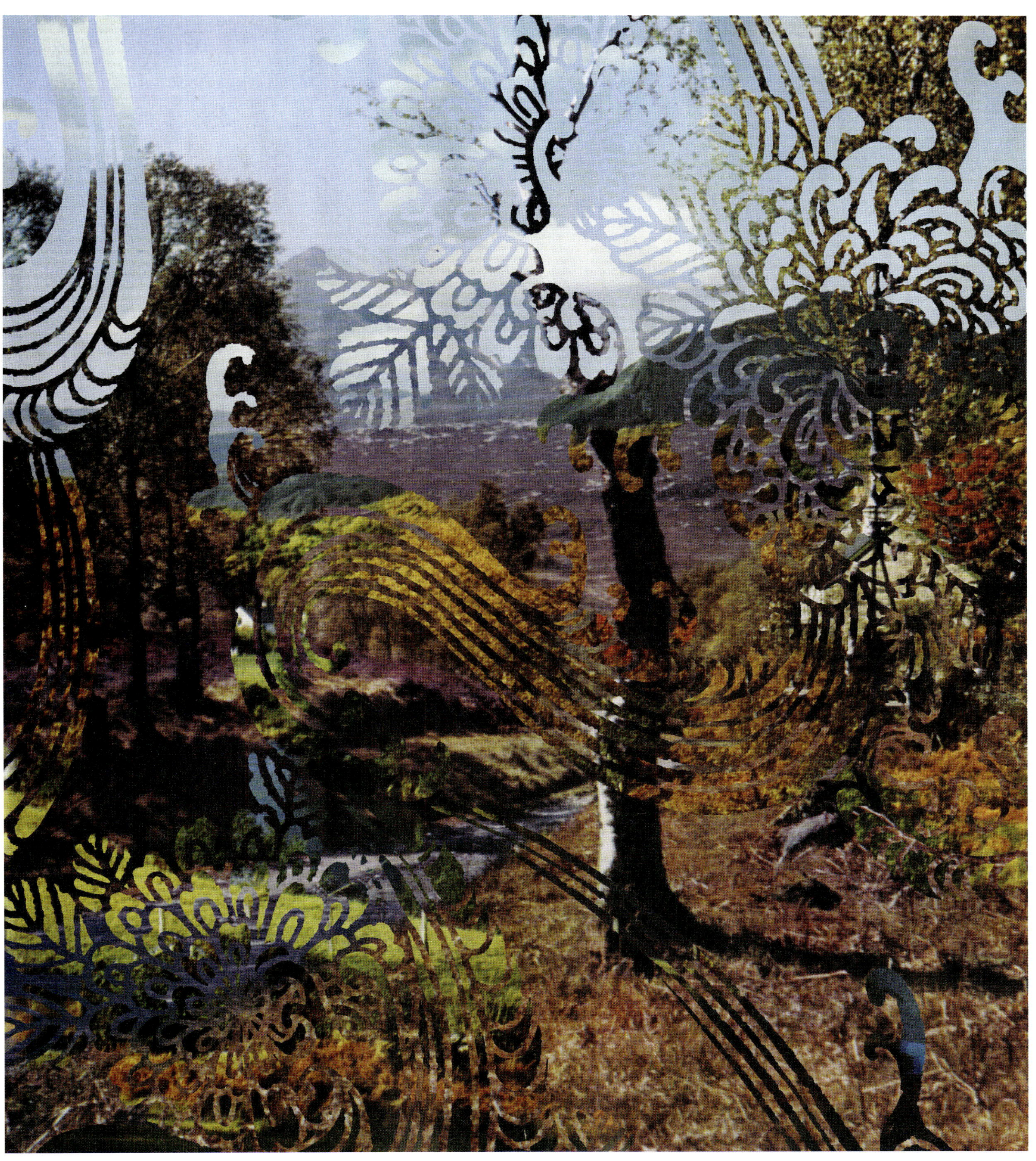

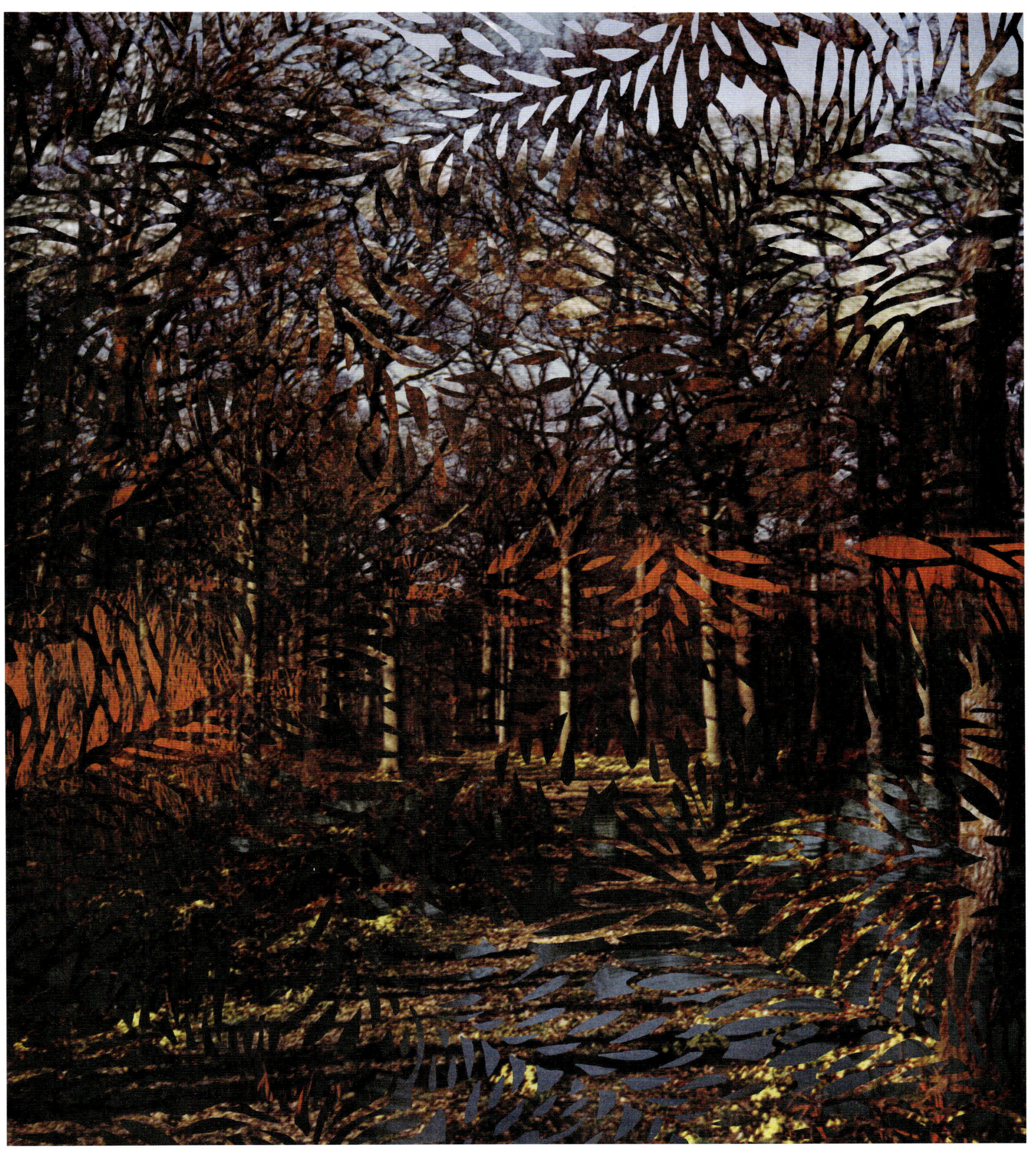

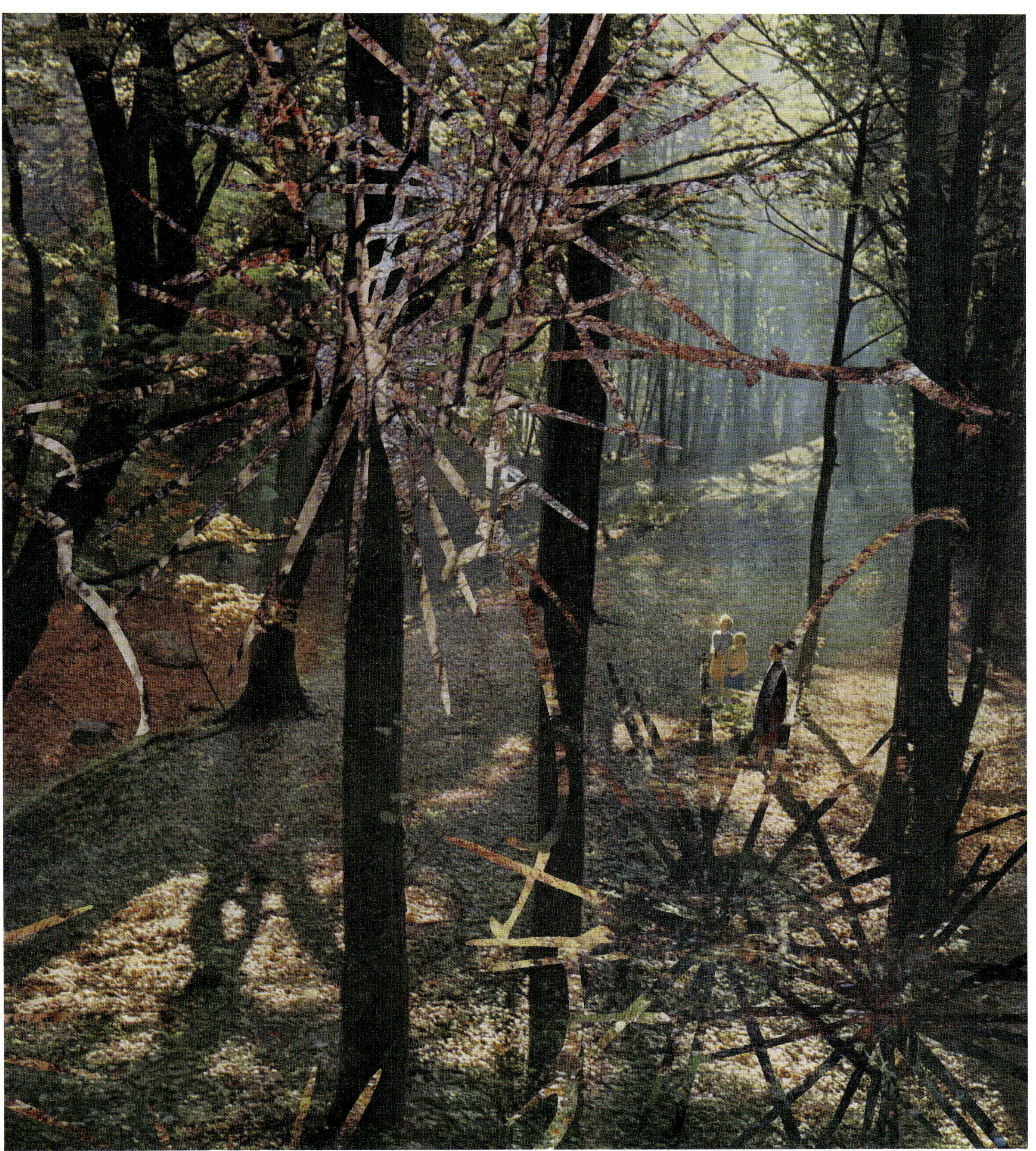

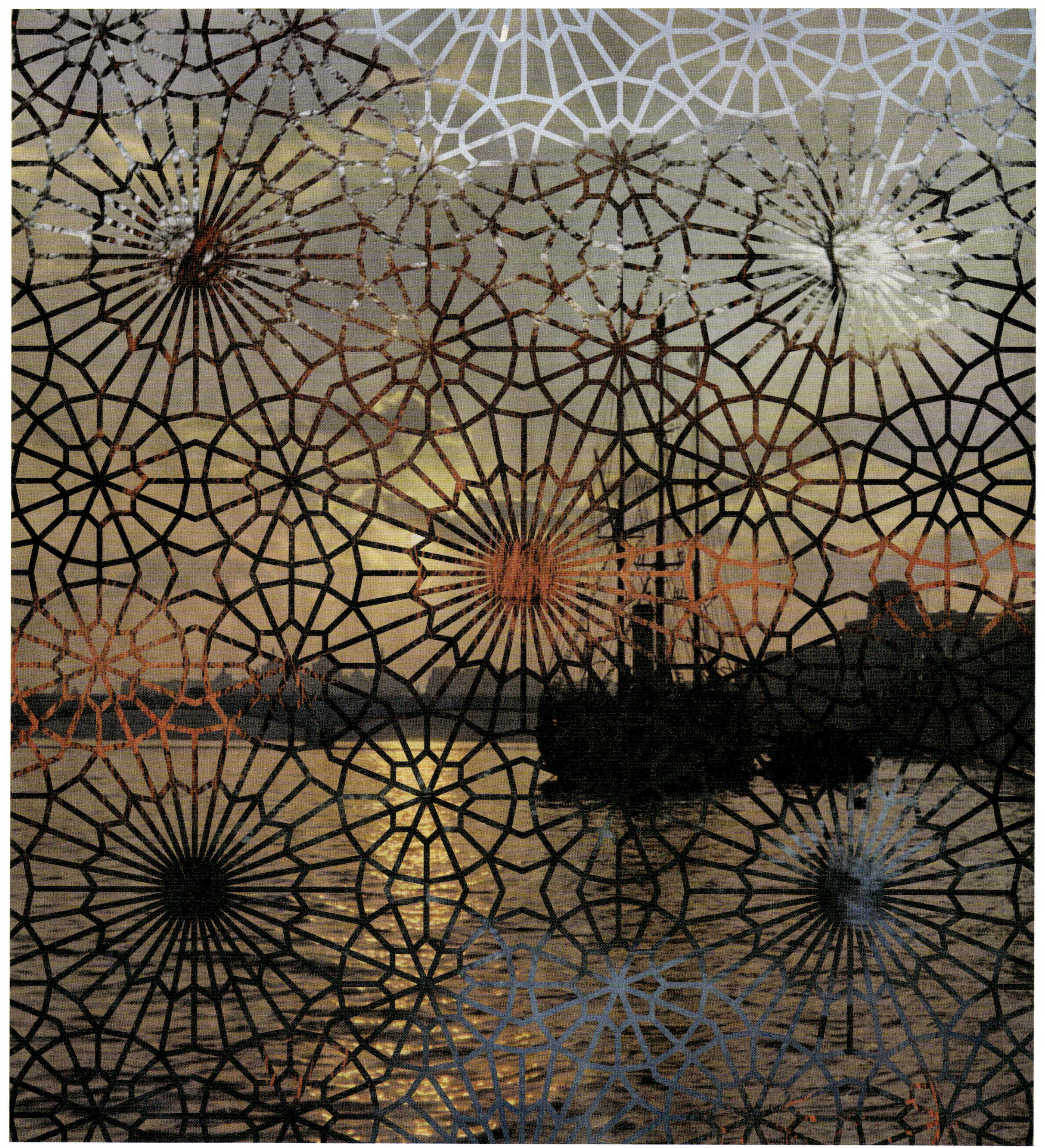

ACKNOWLEDGEMENTS

I would like to thank the following people for their time, help and advice during the course of Henna Nadeem's commission and the production of this book:

Verity Slater and all at Arts Council England South East for their continued support; Camilla Costello at the Country Life Picture Library; Ian Leith at the National Monuments Record Archive; Jennifer Veall and Vivienne Grimes at Conran-Octopus; Carol Agar at the Royal Photographic Society; Alex Starkey and Veronica Hitchcock; Colin McKenzie and Caroline Baron at Charleston Farmhouse; Four Corners Photographic; Sebastian Pedley; John Backham; John Gill, Gilane Tawadros, Stuart Croft and Chloe Hoare at Brighton Photo Biennial; Photoworks interns Beth Steddon, Helen Cammock and Emma-Jane Spain for research and production assistance; Dean Pavitt for his superb design and vital contribution to the editing process; and lastly my colleagues at Photoworks, Rebecca Drew, Gordon MacDonald, Benedict Burbridge, Polly Carter and Helen Wade.

I would also extend our sincere thanks to Henna Nadeem for her inspiration, her hard work and commitment, and for being such a pleasure to work with over the last year.

David Chandler
Director

I would like to thank my Mum and Dad, and sisters Humaira, Rayna and Hubeena for their enduring love and good humour; David Chandler, Ben Burbridge and everyone at Photoworks for their commitment and support throughout the project; Dean Pavitt at LOUP for his great work on the design of the book; and the many photographers without whom this book would not have been possible. Finally I'd like to thank everyone who has supported me through the years with friendship and encouragement.

Henna Nadeem

First published 2006

Photoworks
The Depot, 100 North Road,
Brighton, BN1 1YE
T: 01273 607500
F: 01273 607555
E: info@photoworksuk.org
www.photoworksuk.org

Copyright Note:
Every effort has been made to trace the photographers whose pictures – originally published in Country Life's *Picture Book of Britain* series – have been used as the basis for Henna Nadeem's work in this publication. Although no contacts have been established with the particular photographers concerned, Photoworks wishes to gratefully acknowledge the work of the following people and agencies, without whose effort, vision and superb photographs this book would not have been possible: G. F. Allen, A. C. K. Ware, Aerofilms, A. W. Kerr, A. J. Page, O and J Seed, J. C. Gilchrist, Bill E. Jordan, H. Smith, J. Allen Cash, S. A. Gladstone, Kenneth Scowen, Mirrorpic, E. W. Tattersall, E. Cecil Kerwin, E. A. Bowness, Ian Gilchrist, G. Douglas Bolton, H. Smith, Cecil Curwin, Hugh Sibley, Topical Press, H. L. M. Butcher, G. E. Meacher, Bernard Seed, Howard Edwards.

Editorial team: David Chandler, Henna Nadeem, Benedict Burbridge, Dean Pavitt
Designed by Dean Pavitt at LOUP
Printed in Great Britain by Dexter Graphics Ltd

British Library Cataloguing-in-Publication Data.
A catalogue record for this book is available from the British Library.

ISBN 1-903796-19-9

Distributed by Cornerhouse Publications
70 Oxford Street, Manchester, M1 5NH
T: 0161 200 1503
F: 0161 200 1504
E: publications@cornerhouse.org

Photoworks is an independent arts organisation that brings an international perspective to promoting photography in the South East of England. Photoworks operates over four main areas of activity: commissioning new work, producing exhibitions, publishing books and a twice-yearly magazine, and developing the audience for photography through education and participation programmes.

Henna Nadeem: *A Picture Book of Britain* is published with the support of Arts Council England South East.

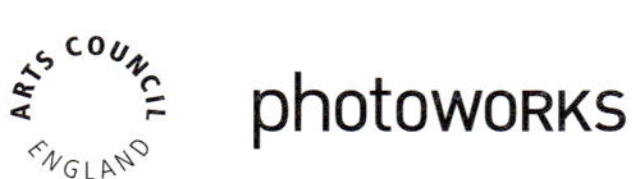